A LONG WAY FROM SOLVING THAT ONE

Psycho/Social and Ethical
Implications of
Ross Macdonald's
Lew Archer Tales

Jeffrey Howard Mahan

UNIVERSITY
PRESS OF
AMERICA

Lanham • New York • London

Copyright © 1990 by
University Press of America®, Inc.
4720 Boston Way
Lanham, Maryland 20706

3 Henrietta Street
London WC2E 8LU England

Library of Congress Cataloging-in-Publication Data

Mahan, Jeffrey H.
A long way from solving that one : psycho/social and
ethical implications of Ross Macdonald's Lew Archer
tales / by Jeffrey Howard Mahan.
p.   cm.
Includes bibliographical references.
1. Macdonald, Ross, 1915–   —Criticism and interpretation.
2. Detective and mystery stories, American—History
and criticism.   3. Archer, Lew (Fictitious character).   4. Social
psychology in literature.   5. Social ethics in literature.   I. Title.
PS3525.I486Z77   1990   813'.52—dc20   89–29561 CIP

ISBN 0–8191–7710–5 (alk. paper)

For Robert P. Mahan

"The Problem was to love people, to serve
them without wanting anything from them.
I was a long way from solving that one."

Lew Archer,
The Barbarous Coast

Table of Contents

PREFACE

The preface provides the author the opportunity to 1) set this study of Ross Macdonald's Lew Archer stories in the context of other works in the area of religion and popular culture, and 2) explain the emphasis placed on the generic context of Macdonald's Work, as well as to 3) acknowledge the influence and contribution of others to this study.

1) Religion and Popular Culture

This section of the introduction serves to outline the history of academic interest in popular culture on which the present study rests.

A Definition of Popular Culture

Though "culture" is properly understood to refer to the totality of behaviors, artistic expressions, beliefs, and institutions transmitted by a society, the phrase "popular culture" is used more narrowly. Those interested in the popular arts have generally used the term "popular culture" to refer to entertainments prepared and marketed for a mass audience. This usage follows the practice of those who use the term "culture" to refer to the forms of social and artistic expression unique to a particular society. Popular novels, films, and television programs are the most obvious forms in which popular culture reaches its audience. One might expand the list to include magazines, popular music, and advertising. Some have further expanded the list to include virtually any item or practice expressive of mass society. This iconic approach to popular culture, which has included studies of phenomena like the automobile and fast food restaurants, has the potential to be informative, but the predominant approach has been to see popular culture studies as a form of narrative analysis and so to limit its study to those objects which unambiguously tell stories.

The Study of Popular Culture

Some would ask, why study Popular culture. But the novels, films, and television shows which make up so much of mass entertainment provide a forum in which social values, attitudes, and relationships are expressed and examined. Treated as shared fantasies, these tales give us insight into the societal unconscious.

The study of American popular culture has usually involved the analysis of the critic's own culture or, more accurately, the culture of people of another class within the critic's society. This has made the work particularly subject to manipulation because of the critical assumptions and cultural biases of the analyst. This problem is compounded by the fact that it is only recently that popular culture has attracted serious scholarly attention.

The traditional attitude of the humanities has tended to be that popular culture is made up of lesser, low-brow works. The scholar's attentions have been directed to the study of those mimetic works culturally affirmed as high culture, and to the introduction of their students to those works.

Social scientists have been more willing to consider popular culture as part of an analysis of mass society, especially within the study of mass communications. But their interests have been predominately with the news and information function, and on "media effects" narrowly understood, rather than on the analysis of the cultural patterns given expression in popular fictions and their meaning for the audience.

Class prejudices may play a role in limiting the serious attention given to popular culture. An interest in popular culture usually needs to be justified in academic circles. There exists a tendency in western society to divide texts between the

individualistic work, which is presumed to reveal the author's vision when studied, and the formulaic work which is presumed to lack such vision, and thus to be an unfit subject for study. This rests on the questionable assumption that meaning is something that the author, who is presumed to be a superior being, inserts into the text. But, as Norman Holland said, "Clearly, meaning is not simply 'there' in the text; rather it is something we construct for the text within the limits of the text."[1] Learning about ourselves and the world around us is a product of the relationship between the "reader" and the "text"[2] rather than the discovery of something that the author has inserted into the text. It rests with the willingness of the reader to ask difficult questions rather than on the difficulty inherent in the text. The popular text is particularly useful to the student of culture both because its broader audience make it potential data for the study of mass (rather than elite) society and because its generic form reveals, not only the vision of a single authorial voice, but a cultural compendium.

The distinction between the high-brow and low-brow arts (which Cawelti less judgmentally defined as "mimetic" and "formulaic"[3]) may not be as easy to make as some have assumed. Many works subsequently judged mimetic, including those of Shakespeare and

---

[1]Norman N. Holland, Dynamics of Literary Response (New York: W.W. Norton & Company, Inc., 1968), p. 25.

[2]"Text" is used throughout the dissertation to refer to the popular work regardless of the medium in which it is presented. Thus we may speak of film, video, or audio texts as well as print texts. Similarly, "reader" refers to the consumer of the text regardless of the text's medium. Popular genres are not normally limited by medium. The mystery story has been presented in books, magazines, films, radio and television formats. Popular tales, or charcters such as Dashiell Hammett's Sam Spade, may be translated into any or all of these media. The Macdonald novels chosen for study here have been translataed into films.

[3]Cf John G. Cawelti, Chapter 1, "The Study of Literary Formulas," in Adventure, Mystery, and Romance (Chicago: University of Chicago Press, 1976).

Dickens,[4] were created for the popular media of their day. Unfortunately, the awareness of this has led some critics to attempt to justify particular popular works as exceptional and timeless. It is unlikely that we have arrived at clear and lasting aesthetic standards which allow us to say which contemporary works will have lasting appeal. In any case, the desire to elevate the popular work to classical status takes the tale out of its generic and societal context and deals with it as a unique and transcendent object.

The founding of The Journal of Popular Culture in 1967 and the creation of the Popular Culture Association (P.C.A.) in 1971 gave popular culturists a forum for communication and did much to make their work academically legitimate. The association and journal have brought together scholars from a wide range of disciplines which include traditional film department humanists, mass communications social scientists, political scientists, philosophers, sociologists, literary scholars, historians, anthropologists, folklorists, and a few theologians. They have arrived at a loose consensus about what constitutes popular culture that is not reflected in their diverse assumptions about methodology.[5] The egalitarian

---

[4]The desire to justify an interest in the popular arts leads to an incessant citation of these precedents as though they proved the worth of the study of contemporary popular culture. This tendency is well illustrated in the first five pages of Peter Wolfe's Dreamers Who Live Their Dreams (Bowling Green: Popular Press, 1976), in which Wolfe compares Macdonald's work to the novels, poetry, and plays of Dickens, Henry James, Shakespeare, Graham Greene, James Joyce, and T.S. Eliot, as well as the music of Mozart and Haydn. The references are cited here only to indicate the difficulty of judging which works will find lasting aesthetic acceptance, not to prove anything about the respective value of either the contemporary or classical works.

[5]In any discussion of the arts, our attention may be given to the object, the artist (producer), or the audience (consumer). Traditional aesthetics have focused on the axis linking artist to the object. Popular culturists, in contrast, have been interested

attitude of the Association and the fact that, with a few notable exceptions,[6] the association has tended to attract younger scholars without clearly established reputations or methodologies, have added to an informality of method which has allowed much work to remain impressionistic. Serious dialogue about how popular culture is to be studied continues to be needed.

Religion and the Arts

An ambivalence about the arts has long existed within the Christian church and shapes the way the arts are studied by scholars of religion. The icons of the Eastern church, the sculptures and paintings with religious subjects and themes of Western artists (often with church patrons), and the gradual acceptance of music in worship exist in tension with the historic distrust of the arts as divinely forbidden "graven images."[7]

---

in the link betwen the audience and the object. Those trained in the humanities have tended to favor the text end of the equation while social scientists have perhaps slighted the text in favor of conclusions about the audience.

[6]One thinks of: Russel Nye, author of the ground breaking history of American popular culture, _The Unembarressed Muse_ (New York: Dial Press, 1970); Ray Browne, who did so much to found the P.C.A. and, at Bowling Green University, developed the Center for the Study of Popular Culture, and the Popular Press; John G. Cawelti, whose _Adventure, Mystery and Romance_ did much to codify the assumptions and approaches in popular culture studies; and in religion Robert Jewett, whose _Captain America Complex_ (Santa Fe, N.M.: Bear & Comp., 1984) signaled the interest of an established scholar of religion in the study of popular culture.

[7]The reader seeking a fuller development of the history of the church's relationship to the arts will find helpful Samuel Laeuchli's _Religion and Art in Conflict_ (Philadelphia: Fortress Press, 1980).

Where there has been an interest in the arts by scholars of religion, it has traditionally focused on the analysis of those works culturally confirmed as "high culture." This approach can be seen in the religion and the arts movement of the last thirty to forty years. Dance, drama, and the graphic arts were brought into the church. Preaching and discussion often focused on the theological structures and themes to be found in what was called "serious literature." An interest in the arts was justified by the revelation of what was often regarded as hidden or latent religious content. Nathan Scott has been one of the most articulate voices in developing a heightened sensitivity to the interaction between the traditions of religion and art in western culture.[8] Valuable as this renewed awareness has been, when the relationship between the arts and Christian faith is assumed to surface out of intellectual activity, it is only able to address the concerns and worship life of a relatively narrow and class-bound range of believers.

Religion and Popular Culture

Some students of religion have found a place for themselves in the cross-disciplinary community of scholars interested in popular culture. They join with colleagues from other fields in rejecting the assumption that popular entertainments are meaningless. Gerald E. Forshey writes, ". . . These entertainments create a mythic world for the individual and society in which human limits and possibilities are shaped, ordered, and given meaning.[9] They share with those from other fields at the Popular Culture Association the basic assumption that popular culture expresses widely shared understandings and fantasies which reveal

---

[8]Scott's work includes: The Broken Center: Studies in the Theological Horizon of Modern Literature (New Haven: Yale University Press, 1966), Craters of the Spirit: Studies in the Modern Novel, (Washington: Corpus Books, 1968), Modern Literature and the Religious Frontier (New York: Harper and Row, 1968).

[9]Gerald E. Forshey, "Studies in Religion and Popular Culture," explor, VII, (Fall 1984), 17.

much about American culture, its values, attitudes, and anxieties.

The religion and the arts movement sought an ideal link between the Christian gospel and cultural expression. In contrast, those working in the area of religion and popular culture have focused on the everyday expressions of the interaction between society and the gospel.

The sociological concern which shapes this work makes it as much a part of the study of religion and mass-society as of traditional theological aesthetics. Students of religion and popular culture sometimes examine the use within popular culture of traditional religious figures and images.[10] At other times the focus is on less overtly religious materials as a form of civil religion.[11] Whatever their focus, the scholars of religion have been somewhat more likely than others of the Popular Culture Association to raise ethical issues and draw moral conclusions about the effects of popular culture on society.[12]

2) The Emphasis on Literary Genre

A problem in using literary approaches to the study of popular culture has been the complexity of the texts and their relationship to the audience. How shall we know what aspect of any particular text - the style of its presentation, the expression of some archetypal pattern, the presentation of a

---

[10]Gerald E. Forshey, "The Apocalyptic Mood in Contemporary Film," explor, IV, (Spring, 1978), pp. 28-37.

[11]John Wiley Nelson, Your God is Alive and Well and Appearing in Popular Culture (Philadelphia: Westminster, 1976).

[12]Ed Berkman, "Superheroes, Antiheroes and the Heroism Void in Children's Television," The Christian Century, XCVI (July 4, 1979), p. 704; also Robert Jewett and John Sheldon Lawrence, American Monomyth (New York: Doubleday, 1977).

protagonist with whom the audience may identify, the attitudes expressed by the author or characters toward some societal group, or any number of other features - is responsible for its appeal?

Genre Studies

The concept of narrative genres has provided a context within which to examine the popular text. By identifying a specific genre (the social melodrama, horror tale, Western, etc.), the critic can narrow the scope of the study and thereby identify recurring patterns, or conventions which seem to be necessary for audience satisfaction. This approach also encourages the critical reader to be aware of changes in the conventions which may point to changes in cultural relationships, attitudes, or values.[13]

A distinctive feature of popular culture studies has been that relatively little attention has been paid to individual creators. The primary focus of scholarly attention has been on the result of interaction, in the marketplace, of creators and consumers of popular tales which produces the patterns which constantly redefine the genres. Where, as with the present study, a particular author is discussed, the author should be regarded primarily as an organizing concept which unites a series of texts rather than as a subject for biographical interest and veneration. For the critical reader, the phrase "Ross Macdonald" indicates a series of texts within the detective genre about which we assume a certain unity of form, style, and subject matter rather than the individual, Kenneth Millar, who happened to write those texts. This ideal has not been entirely realized in the work of popular culturists. But hopefully the interest in Millar's childhood, nationality, and education grows out of a desire to see how a study of the author's life might inform our study of the tales rather than the opposite.

---

[13]This examination of changes in convention led to my observations about how changes in the Western reflected changing attitudes toward modern society in _explor_, VII, (Fall, 1984), pp. 81-93.

3) Acknowledgements

The work in this book appeared in somewhat different form in the dissertation for which I was granted the Ph.D. in the Joint degree program at Northwestern University and Garrett-Evangelical Theological Seminary in 1986. Chapter One appeared with some changes, under the title "The Hardboiled Detective in the Fallen World," in a publication of the Popular Culture Association: <u>Clues</u> I, fall/winter, 1980. It appears here with the kind permission of the editor, Ms Pat Browne. Citations from the work of Ross Macdonald appear with the permission of Alfred A. Knopf, Inc.

I am especially grateful for the guidance and encouragement of my advisor through two degrees, Garrett-Evangelical Dean, Richard D. Tholin and to Northwestern University professor Stuart M. Kaminsky, who played a far more active role than is typical of Northwestern members of Joint University Degree committees and I am indebted to him for the challenge he provided, and for his interest and friendship. Thanks are also due to: my friend and colleague Dr. Gerald Forshey, who introduced me to the Popular Culture Association and the work of those interested in religion and popular culture, to my father, Robert P. Mahan, and my friend Dorothy Philips both of whom read the entire manuscript and provided innumerable stylistic suggestions. Finally, the work would never have been completed without the patience, support, and concern of my wife, The Rev. Louise Mahan, and our son Jason Hoogerhyde.

INTRODUCTION

This book examines several of Ross Macdonald's
Lew Archer novels from the perspective of one interested
in the study of religion and society. The work
presented here grows out of a series of questions
about popular entertainments and their role in
society: How does popular culture function? What
is its relationship to underlying social values?
Is popular culture a radical or conservative force
in society; that is, does it primarily conserve
traditional values and relationships or introduce
new values and relationships? And, how do these
mass-market entertainments serve the needs and
interests of particular segments of society?

This introduction 1) identifies the
cross-disciplinary method used in this study, 2)
considers briefly the Ross Macdonald's place within
the genre and nature of Macdonald's protaganist,
Lew Archer, and 3) provides an outline of this study.

1) A Cross-disciplinary Method

In interpreting the tales our interest is in
their latent and manifest meanings and in how the
audience uses and understands them. In order to
understand the cultural dynamics involved, the work
is shaped by the methodologies of key figures in
theological ethics, psychoanalysis, and sociology.

The choice of a methodology determines the
questions to be asked and thus shapes the final
interpretation of a text. Because drawing on
methods from several fields raises a wider range of
questions it holds out the potential for a richer
reading of the cultural text than would any single
method. Noting the value of a cross-disciplinary
reading does not argue for a study without limits.
The critic must establish manageable limits to the
number of texts to be studied and the methods to be
applied or the task becomes encyclopedic. This
study Ross Macdonald's hard-boiled fiction may
provide some hints of the social function of

mystery fiction in general, and of how popular culture should be understood as a social phenomena. But the primary purpose of this study is more narrowly defined. Can questions rooted in psychoanalytic theory and a particular model of theological ethics help us understand the social function of a particular set of mystery texts?

Novelist Eudora Welty's New York Times essay, "The Stuff that Nightmares are Made Of,"[1] did much to establish Macdonald critical reputation as a serious novelist whose work explored important themes within the mystery genre. This reputation, rather than being the justification for our interest in Macdonald, is but one more piece of information which helps us to see the relationship between the text and its audience. Our task is to see the tale in its cultural context, and thus to determine its social function.[2]

Each of these approaches to understanding the social utility of Macdonald's tales involves the application of the insights of particular representatives of a field to the study of the selected Macdonald texts. Obviously no single figure can reflect the full breadth of a field of study, but theological ethicist H. Richard Niebuhr and psychoanalyst Sigmund Freud were selected for their interest in cultural dynamics. Niebuhr's insight into the form of popular ethical debate and the relationship of particular cultural values to ultimate values makes him a particularly useful representative of theological ethics. Freud's attention to the psychological impact of cultural life and the fact that he actually wrote about the popular culture of his day recommend the inclusion of some of his insights in this study. Together these approaches should lead to conclusions which would not emerge from a study informed by any single method.

---

[1]Book Section, p 7., February 4, 1971.

[2]I am particularly indebted to Robert K. Merton's discussion of "social function" in Social Theory and Social Structure (New York: The Free Press, 1968) for his careful explication of the concept of social function.

It should be understood that, while the questions about the cultural function of popular culture raised in this study are social in nature, the methodology is literary.[3] That is, rather than conduct audience research, the author has made close textual readings. While the approach is based on literary readings, those readings are informed by questions of an explicitly cultural nature which grow out of the consideration of particular examples of theological ethics, psychology, and sociology.

2) The Author, The Genre and The Hero

In the present work, Ross Macdonald's Lew Archer tales are examined as a development of the American "hard-boiled" detective story. This genre, has long been popular in print, on the radio and television, and in the movies. Unlike the Western, which may no longer be adaptable to the needs of a broad audience, the detective story continues to find a wide audience today. The detective story has been well studied and there exists a critical consensus about its form

---

[3]This literary approach to popular culture (at least tacitly) acknowledges that popular culture is a phenomenon of mass society. The critic attempts by literary means to understand its psychological, anthropological, or sociological meanings. Certainly this is the method of those trained in the popular culture program at Bowling Green University or by John Cawelti at the University of Chicago. The present work differs from such works primarily in that it surfaces the questions of cultural meaning and function more explicitly than most.

and conventions.[4] But there remains much to be said about the genre as a moral and social fantasy.

The hard-boiled detective story emerged in the United States as a form of the adventure story typically set in the American metropolis. Its conventions are discussed in some detail in Chapter I. These things make the genre a fitting example through which to pursue a study of popular culture's role in American society. The choice of Ross Macdonald's Lew Archer tales narrows the range to an example accepted by scholars and the mass audience as clearly within the genre, but which seem to be especially popular with a particular subgroup of the larger mystery reading public.

Ross Macdonald was the pen name of Kenneth Millar (December 13, 1915 - July 11, 1983). The Oedipal myth is evident thoughout Macdonald's fiction, which is most often about the effect of parental failings upon subsequent generations. Macdonald's tales are told in the first person by detective Lew Archer.[5] He is a hero made lonely by both his ethical standard and personal history. Archer's expectation of himself judges the failure to create meaningful community of the families he becomes involved with, and indeed of society itself.

In the study of a canon as wide as Macdonald's, the critic must inevitably balance interest in the canon as a whole against the ability to offer careful

---

[4]Cf. The Art of the Mystery Story, ed. Howard Haycraft (New York: Simon and Schuster, 1946); George Grella's often anthologized "Murder and the Mean Streets: The Hard Boiled Detective Novel," Contempora, March 1970; and Cawelti, Adventure, Mystery, and Romance. The reader interested in the attention given the mystery story by modern psychological and structural critics such as Penderson-Krag, Lacan, Eco, and Barthes will find helpful The Poetics of Murder, eds. Glenn W. Most and William W. Stowe (New York: Harcourt Brace Jovanovich, 1983).

[5]Jerry Speir creates a biography for the detective from bits and pieces of background in the novels which can be found in Ross Macdonald (New York: Frederick Ungar, 1978) p. 109f.

examination of individual works. A manageably sized
consideration of each of Macdonald's novels would
inevitably treat each superficially. The problem
in choosing examples is how to decide what constitutes
a "typical" example. Since our interest is in the
mass audience, the three Archer novels which have
been adapted for the screen (and thus reached a wider
and more general audience than does the mystery novel)
have been chosen and are examined in some detail.
The reader particularly interested in the process
of adaption for the screen, or of how that adaptive
process has shaped the Archer tales, will want to
turn to the Appendix titled "From Novel to Film."

3) Outline of the Present Work

Chapter One, The Morality of the Hard-boiled Detective
in a Fallen World reviews the history of this uniquely
American form of the mystery story. The social vision
of the genre and the moral problems presented through
the detective protagonist and his tale are presented.
This provides a historical context for the analysis
of Macdonald which follows.

Chapter Two, Ego Control and Independence in THE
MOVING TARGET uses Freud's reflections on the popular
culture of his day and his analysis of the way
conflicting forces within the individual affect the
struggle to find one's place in society to reveal
the way these tensions are expressed in popular
culture. Macdonald's fiction expresses and
resolves in fantasy conflicts which the reader
experiences both within the unconscious and in
interaction with others.

Chapter Three, The Ethics of Responsibility in THE
UNDERGROUND MAN uses H. Richard Niebuhr's suggestion
that responsibility has become the dominant contemporary
ethical model to provide a framework for the literary
examination of Macdonald's most critically acclaimed
work. This examination of moral decision-making
reveals the way in which Macdonald's fiction addresses
the question of what it means to be a moral individual
in the world, and the way the absence of a monotheistic
center limits Macdonald's ability to radically critique
his society.

Chapter Four, Conclusions, The Psycho/Social and Ethical Implications of the Archer Tales shows how an awareness of Niebuhr's perspective on radical monotheism makes explicit the relative absence of monotheistic commitment in most popular culture. It is suggested that this absence combines with others pressures so that hard-boiled detective fiction tends to serve society by preserving traditional values and concepts and reducing the conflict between traditional and emerging values. In so doing, the genre's predominant impact is conservative. Macdonald's Archer tales fulfill this function in ways which serve the unique needs of the intellectual class.

The Appendix, From Novel to Film explores the differences between print and film, novel and movie, and considers the audience's expectation of each. The issues and problems inherent in the translation of a narrative work from one medium to another are exlored. The choices made in adapting each of the three Archer novels which have been filmed are considered.

CHAPTER ONE
THE MORALITY OF THE HARD-BOILED DETECTIVE
IN A FALLEN WORLD

Throughout the present work Ross Macdonald's fiction is treated as a development of the hard-boiled detective story. His work is assumed to exist in relationship to the conventions of that genre. This is not to suggest that Macdonald is somehow a lesser artist who lacks a personal vision or style; rather it is a reminder that literature is a cultural product which responds to culturally determined conventions. Whether an author follows, or reacts against, the aesthetic assumptions of his or her culture, those assumptions shape the work. This is true of the poet who learns to write sonnets or free verse as well as the writer of mysteries. The detective story, like all literature, has a history which shapes its form and content. The conventions of formulaic stories, such as the social melodrama, Western, and detective story may be more readily apparent than are those of the mimetic tale, but the difference is of degree, not kind. This chapter: 1) traces the development of the hard-boiled detective story, 2) considers its assumptions about the world, 3) explores the social and ethical assumptions expressed within such stories, and 4) concludes by placing Macdonald's work within the framework of the genre within which he chooses to work.

1) The Development of the Hard-Boiled Detective Story

A distinctive variation of the mystery story developed in the American pulp magazines of the 1920's.[1] Black Mask is the publication usually credited with being the birthplace of the new form that came to

---

[1]Those anxious to know more about the development of the pulps, named for the cheap paper stock on which they were printed, will find helpful the issue of Clues, II (Fall/Winter, 1981) subtitled "Focus on Pulp Detective Fiction."

be called hard-boiled detective fiction.[2] By combining elements of the adventure and mystery formulas, the detective tale was changed from an intellectual puzzle to a tale of manly action and moral self definition. When Macdonald placed early short stories at Black Mask, he followed in the footsteps of Carroll John Daley (author of the Race Williams stories), Dashiel Hammett (the Continental Op, and Sam Spade), and Raymond Chandler (Philip Marlowe). The "Black Mask" writers and their audience did much to establish the conventions of the genre, which in turn shaped the work of the creators of subsequent novels, films and popular television series from the days of Peter Gunn to contemporary series like Spencer for Hire.

This widely popular variation of the mystery story differs from the classical story of detection, not only in its plot conventions, but also in its assumptions about the world. The classical story brings an element of disruption into an otherwise orderly world. The task of the detective in an Agatha Christie or Conan Doyle story is to restore the world to its natural and uncorrupted state. As the hard-boiled story progresses we discover that evil is increasingly revealed to be endemic and contagious. The natural state of the hard-boiled world is corrupt and the imago Dei becomes an image seen in a fun house mirror.

The hard-boiled detective does not defend the orderly society of the classical story but a private code of honor which sets him apart from the world he lives in. It seems an interesting paradox that it is precisely the high demand that he places on his own character which alienates the hard-boiled detective from his world. In such stories, the modern city becomes a dark and frightening place. Macdonald, like so many other writers of hard-boiled fiction, chooses a darkly viewed Los Angeles as the archetype of that city.

---

[2] For a review of the role of Black Mask in founding the hard-boiled detective story see "The Black Mask School" by Philip Durham, which first appeared in Tough Guy Writers of the Thirties, ed. David Madden, and is reprinted in The Mystery Writer's Art, ed. Francis M. Nevins, Jr., (Bowling Green: Popular Press, 1970), pp. 197 ff.

The Problem of Realism

Raymond Chandler suggests that what distinguishes the hard-boiled story from the traditional detective story is its realism. In his essay "The Simple Art of Murder,"[3] and in his published correspondence,[4] Chandler argues against the exotic murders for bizarre reasons of the Murder on the Orient Express variety. "Hammett gave murder back to the kind of people that commit it for reasons, not just to provide a corpse; and with the means at hand, not with hand-wrought duelling pistols, curare, and tropical fish."[5] This, the grittiness of the hard-boiled city, and the social class of the protagonists seem to be the realism of which Chandler speaks.

It is interesting that Chandler is drawn to define the genre in terms of reality. Certainly both he and writers of the classical tradition like Agatha Christie have created sharply defined worlds within which certain characters and events seem more reasonable than others. American taste and literary convention may suggest that the cities of California and the potentially tragic adventures of a marginally middle class detective are more "real" than the trans-European railway, an effete Belgian detective, or an elderly gentlewoman in her English village. But the literary Los Angeles of Raymond Chandler and Ross Macdonald is as much an artistic creation as the London of Arthur Conan Doyle and Dick Francis. The preference of one over the other tells us more about the assumptions of the audience than the world they inhabit. One has only to read Hammett's The Maltese Falcon with its strange villians and unlikely quest to realize that the hard-boiled world is as

---

[3]Raymond Chandler, "The Simple Art of Murder" in Detective Fiction: Crime and Compromise, D. Allen and D. Chacko eds. (New York: Harcourt, Brace, Jovanovich, 1974), pp. 387-399.

[4]Raymond Chandler Speaking, Dorothy Gardiner and Kathrine Sorley Walker, eds. (Boston: Houghton Mifflin Company, 1977).

[5]Chandler, in Allen and Chacko, p. 396.

fanciful as that of the classical story. Chandler, himself, acknowledged that "This realism is superficial; the potential of emotion is overcharged, the compression of time and event is a violation of probability."[6]

I suspect that what leads Chandler and other to argue for the "realism" of the hard-boiled story is not the events that are portrayed. Rather it is the assumptions about human nature and the world out of which the events come that these writers see as more realistic. It is the corruption and greed at the root of the hard-boiled crime that makes it seem more "real" than the classical story's crime. The hard-boiled story assumes that the world is an evil place, that individuals suffer from both hidden and obvious sin, and that civilization is corrupt. What keeps this world view from being finally tragic is the possibility of a hero who can stand against it.

It is this view of the world and the people who live there which most interests the student of religion and culture in the hard-boiled story. These tales see the world in a fallen state and explore how one might live in it. A heroic figure who does not simply surrender to the fallen nature of the world models the possibility of not being co-opted by the world as it is.

2) The Genre's Assumptions About the World

We find the hard-boiled detective at the edge of the city's splendor. He is not an insightful eccentric like the classical story's Sherlock Holmes or Miss Marple but a lower middle-class guy, a "marginal professional."[7] Chandler places Philip Marlowe's office in "a reasonably shabby corridor in the sort

---

[6]Ibid.

[7]John D. Cawelti, Adventure, Mystery, and Romance (Chicago: University of Chicago Press, 1976), p. 144.

of building that was new about the year the all-tile
bathroom became the basis of civilization."[8]

Cawelti describes the hard-boiled detective's
setting as "the kind of office associated with unsuc-
cessful dentists, small mail order businesses, and
shyster lawyers."[9] Indeed Stuart Kaminsky places
his detective, Toby Peters, in an office shared with
a skid row dentist.[10] It is in such places that
we meet the hardboiled detective, for his place defines
his relationship to the city and thus his character.
The unwillingness to go along with corruption keeps
the hard-boiled detective from a worldy success and
so we find him at the outskirts of the city's business
district, made poor by his ideals.

The hard-boiled detective's physical poverty
is like that of a saint, revealing both his moral
superiority and his separation from the world. He
may appear to have been defeated by the world, but
in actuality he has chosen his place. The choice
is made clear in the hard-boiled detective's rejection
of the world's offer to profit by going along with
the corruption which he comes up against. Lew Archer's
refusal of Walter Kilbourne's bribe in The Drowning
Pool,[11] like Sam Spade's refusal to join Guttman
in his quest for the black bird near the end of The
Maltese Falcon,[12] is an obvious example of the
hard-boiled detective's unwillingness to be
bought. He is a rebel who has rejected the success

---

[8]Raymond Chandler, The Midnight Raymond
Chandler (Boston: Houghton Mifflin Company, 1971),
p. 203.

[9]Cawelti, p. 144.

[10]Stuart M. Kaminsky, Bullet for a Star, (New
York: St. Martin's Press, 1977), p. 55. And other
novels.

[11]Ross Macdonald, The Drowning Pool (New
York: Bantam Books, 1970), p. 180.

[12]Dashiel Hammett, The Maltese Falcon (New
York: Vintage Books, 1972), p. 184.

that he sees around him. Where the respectable are corrupt, he has chosen a way that is neither respectable nor successful.

The contrast between the independence of the hero and the limitations of the police is a convention of hard-boiled fiction. Commonly, the hard-boiled detective has been a police officer who has left the force or been fired. Lew Archer for instance, like Chandler's Philip Marlowe, says in The Moving Target[13] that he once worked for the district attorney. And, in The Way Some People Die,[14] Archer reports having left the Long Beach police force rather than accept graft. This convention amplifies the hard-boiled detective's moral independence. The legal system's limits, inadequacies and corruptions interfere with his search for a personal purity and a piece of justice, so that when we come to know him the hard-boiled detective has already left the force. The tension between the detective and the police is evident when Chandler's Philip Marlowe tells the police:

'Until you guys own your own souls you don't own mine. Until you guys can be trusted everytime and always, in all times and conditions, to seek the truth out and find it and let the chips fall where they may - until that time comes, I have a right to listen to my conscience, and protect my client the best way I can. '[15]

The moral individual moves away from societal institutions in hard boiled fiction because such a person can never be at ease with the ethical compromise that the institution inevitably makes.

---

[13] Ross Macdonald, The Moving Target (New York: Bantam, 1979), pp. 3-4.

[14] John Ross Macdonald, The Way Some People Die (New York: Pocket Books, 1952), p. 112.

[15] Raymond Chandler, The High Window (New York: Vintage Books, 1976), p. 92.

The Detective's World and Ours

From his shabby office, or his equally shabby apartment, the hard-boiled detective ventures forth into the fallen world that surrounds him. There, among the people who live in it, we experience the dark realism that sets the hard-boiled story apart from the classical story's neat puzzles. The hard-boiled detective inhabits an empty world of neon, valueless modernity, and death. Chandler writes:

> The realist in murder writes of a world in which gangsters can rule nations and almost rule cities, . . . where no man can walk down a dark street in safety because law and order are things we talk about but refrain from practising; a world where you may witness a hold-up in broad daylight and see who did it, but you will fade quickly back into the crowd rather than tell anyone, because the hold-up men may have friends with long guns, or the police may not like your testimony, and in any case the shyster for the defense will be allowed to abuse and vilify you in open court, before a jury of selected morons, without any but the most perfuctory interference from a political judge.
>
> It is not a very fragrant world, but it is the world you live in,...[16]

Chandler moves from the corruption of the powerful to the cowardice it brings out in us. We become corrupted by our inaction in a world where others act evilly. Thus Chandler tells us that the world of the hard-boiled detective is the world we inhabit. Only after he has established that the detective's corrupt world is our own does Chandler bring in the possibility of a hero who could stand against the world's corruption.

But down these mean streets a man must go who is not himself mean, who is neither tarnished nor afraid.[17]

---

[16]Raymond Chandler, "The Simple Art of Murder," in Allen and Chacko, pp. 387-99.

[17]Ibid., p. 398.

This often quoted line from the same article defines the hard-boiled detective by his journey through the world. That journey at once reveals the fallen nature of the world and suggests the possibility of a small and personal triumph by the hero who sees the world as it is and remains uncorrupted.

The World Revealed

Someone comes to the hard-boiled detective out of that world seeking help. In Raymond Chandler's Farewell, My Lovely, it happens as he is passing a tavern door:

> A hand I could have sat in came out of the dimness and took hold of my shoulder and squashed it to a pulp. Then the hand moved me through the doors and casually lifted me up a step.[18]

More often, as in Chandler's The Little Sister, Hammett's The Maltese Falcon, and the Macdonald novels studied here, someone seeks out the detective and asks for help. She (for it is usually a woman) describes a crime which threatens her and the detective goes forth to confront it.

The crime does not sit still and wait for the hardboiled detective to solve it as does the already accomplished crime of the typical classical tale. Rather, it unfolds around him, often requiring him to move from the apparent issue to a real and underlying problem. This uncertainty about the actual issue and lack of all the facts plunges the detective into a murky world where it becomes hard to make neat moral distinctions.

The Maltese Falcon provides an example of this. Brigid O'Shaughnessy comes to the detectives, Spade and Archer, under an assumed name (Miss Wonderly) claiming that she wants help in locating a non-existent sister. Several names and stories later, Sam Spade is in the middle of a drama that no one will fully explain to him. Only by piecing together the stories of all concerned and by reflecting on the holes in

---

[18]Raymond Chandler, The Raymond Chandler Omnibus (New York: Knopf, 1975), p. 144.

their stories can he come to understand the real issues.

In the beginning, the detective finds corruption in the places one expects to find it, among the gangsters and petty criminals who prey on society. As the story progresses, the detective is forced to see that the problem is not to be found simply in a few bad people but in the nature of the world. The deeper he digs the more broadly based the corruption is revealed to be. The limitations of the police are seen, and then we may find that the police and the courts are corrupt.

Theologian and ethicist Reinhold Niebuhr describes a similar separation between the moral individual and the society. Niebuhr advances the argument by seeing human duplicity as the key to the separation between the two:

> The inevitable hypocrisy, which is associated with all of the collective activities of the human race, springs chiefly from this source: that individuals have a moral code which makes the actions of collective man an outrage to their conscience.[19]

The Swiss theologian Karl Barth addressed the nature of the world in his discussion of the point in the Apostles' Creed where we pronounce that our Lord "suffered under Pontius Pilate." In Dogmatics in Outline he writes, "Pilate thus stands for the order which confronts the other order represented by Israel and the Church."[20] As Pilate washes his hands, he represents world history and all of the times that human beings have washed their hands, declining to act out of selfless love for the others, and thus hand the Christ over to be crucified. Yet Pilate is not a uniquely evil man. If he were, the problems would not be so immense. Pilate is ordinary. Because he is like each of us, he reveals something

---

[19]Reinhold Niebuhr, _Moral Man and Immoral Society_ (New York: Charles Scribner's Sons, 1960). pp. 8-9.

[20]Karl Barth, _Dogmatics in Outline_ (New York: Harper & Row, 1959), p. 110.

about us and about the world we have made.   Barth says of Pilate,

> He does what politicians have more or less always done . . . : He attempts to rescue and maintain order in Jerusalem and thereby at the same time to preserve his own position of power, by surrendering the clear law.[21]

And so, as politicians of the hard-boiled detective story attest, things continue to be in the world.

The world of the hard-boiled detective seems remarkably like the fallen world of Christian theology. There is the higher ideal, and the world which never totally allows us to live up the the ideal.   The politicians and the police officers whom the hard-boiled detective meets remind us of Barth's Pontius Pilate, corrupted by the order in which they participate.   Such a world alienates the sensitive conscience and makes lasting relationships with others difficult.

The hard-boiled detective explores the world, experiences it as it is, learns from it and bases his actions on his knowledge of the world.   But, while the detective has a physical competence, it does not allow him to transform his world as the Western hero's does.   In the classical Western, the hero is able to destroy the representative of evil and this transform the world. The detective is seldom able to significantly alter the structures of the world.   Instead, by perserverance and an unfailing insistence on knowing the truth, the detective frees the client to continue to live in the world.

3) Social and Ethical Assumptions

The hard-boiled detective can serve as model because of the relationship his world bears to ours. The "realism" with which the detective's world is described suggests that the corruption of this world is like that of our own.   Therefore a dispossessed and marginal character may suggest, by his struggle to live a moral life, that other people who see themselves as marginalized might also share in the

---

[21]Ibid., p. 111.

10

heroic struggle to stand up to the corruption of the world. The reward that is promised is not the transformation of the world but the salvaged moral character of the individual.

The realistic world of the hard-boiled detective writer can be compared to the Christian understanding of the world as fallen. In both understandings the world encompasses the people who live in it and the forces that shape their lives. Both understandings see the world as the arena in which the individual confronts evil, whether that evil is described as sin or corruption.

The detective bears his burden and takes his blows in order to be true to his code of behavior. He sees the fallenness of the world because to avoid it would be less than honest. In his essay, "Murder and the Mean Streets," George Grella traces this interest of the hard-boiled story to its root in the American novel:

> Influenced by the Puritan imagination, it tends to see life as a Manichean struggle between good and evil; its vision, moreover, is usually obsessed with sin. Energized by the self-reliance of the frontier, it customarily establishes its moral norm within the consciousness of an individual man.[22]

Individual and Social Morality

Reinhold Niebuhr's distinction between what is possible for the moral individual and for society is helpful in understanding the hard-boiled detective. In Moral Man and Immoral Society Reinhold Niebuhr explores the individual and collective ego and considers the way in which the ego may be restrained. He suggests that it is possible for the individual to decline to pursue self-interest and act out of love (i.e., selfless concern) for the other. Because of the less controlled nature of the collective ego, societies are not able to base their actions on love. Self-interest is too powerful in the group and thus justice (the valuing of the other as highly as the

---

[22]George Grella, "Murder and the Mean Streets: The Hard-Boiled Detective Story," in Allen & Chacko, p. 412.

self) is the most that we can hope for as the basis
for a societal morality.

This conflict between society and the sensitive
conscience is made inevitable by the double focus
of the moral life. The requirements of the social
order are never entirely at peace with the inner
life of the individual. At best society will strive
for justice in ways that will offend the loving
conscience. And often the collective ego will assert
itself so that society ceases trying for justice
at all and strives only for its own self interest.

Since society is made up of individuals whose
consciences must be satisfied, society lies to itself
and to the world about the nature of its actions.
At the same time that society acknowledges its self-
interest, it claims that its actions reflect the
society's loving concern for the other. Reinhold
Niebuhr uses the examples of white American slave
owners and British colonizers of India to demonstrate
this principle. Each claimed that they needed the
status quo (and deserved it due to inherent moral
superiority) at the same time they claimed they acted
out of selfless love for those whom they oppressed.

Reinhold Niebuhr demonstrates that society dupes
itself, believing the moral claims it makes to disguise
its self-interest. Thus only an exceptional individual,
or outsider, can reveal the hypocracy of such claims.
The writers of hard-boiled fiction presents the
detective as such an exceptional outsider who
reveals the corruption of the world he inhabits.
Though he knows the modern city well he never quite
belongs. It is this alienation which allows him to
see what others hide from themselves.

The Ethics of The Detective

The deeper the detective pursues the truth
the more endemic the evil of the world becomes.
Those around him become implicated in it and he must
struggle to avoid evil's entrapment. This experience
makes the hard-boiled detective a loner. He may
have passing relations with others, but the more
intimate they become the more likely he is to find
in them the same evil which infects all the others.
Marlowe's friendship with Terry Lenox in The Long
Goodbye or Sam Spade's affair with Brigid O'Shaughnessy

in The Maltese Falcon are archetypal examples of this problem. In each story the person the detective loves best is finally revealed to be the source of the particular corruption with which the story deals.

Sex becomes problematic for the hard-boiled detective. Unlike his classical counterpart, he is likely to become romantically involved with a woman. However, women are both a pleasure and a trap for him. In the classical formula, it is possible for a woman close to the detective to be suspected of a crime and exonerated by the detective. Almost the opposite happens in the hard-boiled story, where the detective is likely to discover in the end that a woman whom he loved and trusted is revealed to be, not the victim, but the villain.[23] Thus at the place of greatest intimacy the hard-boiled detective finds further evidence of the corrupt nature of the world. Perhaps this is what keeps him single.

His insistence on knowing the truth is a part of the hard-boiled detective's moral code which keeps the detective on the job when the client is ready to let things drop and the police or the villains are insisting on his silence. This is a trait we see in Marlowe as well as in Macdonald's Lew Archer. His solutions are not the beautiful, logical constructions of the classical detective, but the product of his stick-to-it-ive-ness. By hanging on, refusing to be bribed, pushed away, or murdered, the detective finally worries his way to a solution. This perseverance becomes a matter of honor for the detective; he is true to a code which no one but the reader seems to understand. This is no riddle, as in the case of the classical detective, and so the question of the price the criminal must pay, of revenge, is correspondingly greater than in the classical tale. In the corrupt world in which the hard-boiled detective lives the law is an inexact instrument and it often fails to produce justice. The police represent the limitations of human institutions, and thus it often falls to the detective to mete out justice.

Consider the final scene of The Maltese Falcon. The blackbird has been revealed to be a fake; Guttman, Cairo, and Wilmur have gone; Sam Spade is left

---

[23]Cawelti, p. 147.

alone with Brigid O'Shaughnessy. He must decide whether to turn in the woman he loves for murdering his partner, whom he didn't particularly like or respect. In a moment which combines the urge to share intimacy and the ideals which prevent him from settling for an imitation of intimacy, Spade struggles with this untenable problem:

> 'I'm going to send you over. The chances are you'll get off with life. That means you'll be out again in twenty years. You're an angel. I'll wait for you. . . .

> When a man's partner is killed he's supposed to do something about it. It doesn't make any difference what you thought of him. He was your partner and you're supposed to do something about it.'

Spade turns to the matter of his love for her:

> 'Now on the other side we've got what? All we've got is the fact that maybe you love me and maybe I love you.'

Knowing that she will not understand he says finally:

> 'If that doesn't mean anything to you forget it and we'll make it this: I won't because all of me wants to . . . .'[24]

The film[25] based on the novel ends as the police take Brigid O'Shaughnessy away in the elevator of Spade's apartment building. The camera lingers on her face as the prison-like doors of the elevator close in front of her and then slowly, as the elevator descends, she drops out of the frame.

Here, in a single scene, we see the essential separation of the hard-boiled detective from the world. We see how the separation grows out of his code of ethics and how he must confront the corruption of the world in those who are closest to him.

---

[24]Hammett, pp. 191-94.

[25]The Maltese Falcon (Warner Brothers, 1941) directed by John Huston.

4) Conclusions

We have in the hard-boiled detective a character who has chosen a way of life that forces him to peer into the dark corners of the world. He receives no worldly reward for this and is reviled, beaten, and forced to see the duplicity of those he loves. Yet this figure functions as a heroic model within the narrative. He remains one who accepts the social alienation that Reinhold Niebuhr suggests is the price of the moral life.

Too much can be made of the similarities between the hard-boiled story's world view and that of neo-orthodox Christian theology. The hard-boiled detective story begins with surviving the immediate threat and extends only to the possibility that the detective may find for his client a limited justice. Eschatology looks forward to the final confrontation between good and evil and thus hopes for a new order in this world or another. It holds a promise of final solutions which the hard-boiled story cannot offer.

Exploring a parallel between Christ and the hard-boiled detective, Grella quotes the line which gives this study its title. "'The problem was to love people, to serve them, without wanting anything from them. I was a long way from solving that one.'"[26] While the parallel is a limited one, it is especially helpful in understanding Philip Marlowe and Lew Archer. Both of these fictional detectives reflect on this strange work of theirs, that seems to consist primarily of suffering for others, in a manner which makes clear that they feel drawn to take on the burdens of others without regard for the possibility of their own profit. Thus, using Reinhold Niebuhr's definition, they are men who act out of love for others.

The realist attitude toward the world is a convention common to all of the hard-boiled stories. If the readers accept this corrupt and fallen world as analogous to their own, then the hard-boiled story becomes a moral fantasy of great appeal. The detective's failure and frustration,

---

[26]Ross Macdonald, _Barbarous Coast_, cited by Grella in Allen & Chacko, p. 417.

15

social position, and ambiguous relationship to the societal elite combine with his masculine courage and integrity to encourage the reader to identify with the detective.[27] We have then in the tale of the hard-boiled detective a popular literature which shares with contemporary theology a concern for how people are to live in the corrupt world and explores the problems through the adventures of an idealized hero.

It has been suggested in this chapter that concern for the moral life shapes the tale of the hard-boiled detective and offers some explanation of its popularity. From here, attention will be focused on a particular example of the genre, Ross Macdonald's Lew Archer novels.

---

[27]Cawelti, pp. 160-61.

CHAPTER TWO
EGO CONTROL AND INDEPENDENCE IN THE MOVING TARGET

Psychology and sociology emerged in the same period. Freud was a contemporary of the great social theorists Max Weber and Emil Durkheim and one might reasonably turn to either social theorist for a model for social analysis. One striking dissimilarity between Freud and the sociologists of his day which may make him particularly helpful in understanding the hard-boiled detective story lies in their differing attitudes toward society. Freud presents the instinctual renunciation required by society to enable human growth and development as a much more difficult process than do the sociologists. Unlike Durkheim, Freud assumes that people don't want society,

> little as men are able to exist in isolation, they ... nevertheless feel as a heavy burden the sacrifices that civilization expects of them in order to make a communal life possible.[1]

Freud believed only the necessity of restraining one's neighbors makes civilization an acceptable compromise for any individual, a social assumption in many ways shared by hard-boiled fiction.

While traditional authorship studies treat the text as the expression of its creator's unique voice, popular culture studies examine the popular text as an articulation of values, attitudes tensions, or anxieties of an entire culture. Because these often exist at an unconscious level in the text, just as they do within an individual, an approach informed by psychology is helpful in understanding the text and its social function.

---

[1]Sigmund Freud, Future of an Illusion, trans. James Strachey (New York: W.W. Norton & Co., 1961), p. 6.

17

The breadth of Sigmund Freud's interests makes him a particularly useful source for the student of popular culture. Freud studied both individual and group psychology and was interested in the psychological forces that shape society. Freud brought a knowledge of the arts to bear on his psychoanalytic studies.

In order to consider whether a Freudian analysis of a popular literary work can reveal cultural values this chapter will: 1) consider the Freudian vision of society, 2) relate Freud's own interpretation of the popular culture of his day to the first of Ross Macdonald's Lew Archer novels - The Moving Target, 3) utililze Freud's description of the conflicts within the personality to analyze narrative tensions within the novel, and 4) draw conclusions about The Moving Target as a form of displaced wish fulfillment.

1) A Freudian Vision of Society

Any narrative involves the creation or presentation of a society, but the hard-boiled tale, with its almost inevitable setting in an American metropolis, seems uniquely able to examine the pressures of life in modern society which so interested Freud.

"Culture" or "civilization" (terms which Freud uses interchangeably) makes possible all of the fruits of human cooperation. Language, art, division of labor, everything that may be regarded as the advancement of the species, is the result of the processes of civilization. But these advances are not without price; men and women do not give themselves easily to society. Civilization demands a high level of individual renunciation to make possible its rewards.

Egocentric human nature makes the regulation of human relationships in society difficult. For even those who recognize the value of civilization seek their own ends before the common good. Freud insisted that for human beings:

> instinctual endowments is to be reckoned a powerful share of aggressiveness. As a result, their neighbor is for them not only a potential helper or sexual object, but also someone who tempts them to satisfy their aggressiveness on him, to exploit his capacity for work without compen-

sation, to use him sexually without his consent, to seize his possisions, to humiliate him, to cause him pain, to torture and to kill him. <u>Homo homini lupus.</u>[2]

The reader of Macdonald should recognize this description of the individual within society.

For Freud, and for Macdonald, <u>society is an imperfect compromise between the demands of instinct and the restrictions and renunciations necessary if we are to live with one another.</u> And the inequalities of society exacerbate the problems. Yet Freud believes that human nature itself undercuts the possibility of any utopian resolution of these problems. He writes, ". . . There are difficulties attaching to the nature of civilization which will not yield to any attempt at reform."[3]

What people seek from life in society is "happiness," that is, the absence of pain and the experience of strong feelings of pleasure. But Freud's model for happiness is orgasmic; it is ". . . only possible as an episodic phenomenon."[4] Civilization is in many ways unpleasant; it forces people to perform tasks they don't want to do, and this is especially true for the poorer classes. Society makes demands on all citizens, but it rewards them unequally for their renunciations. It should not suprise us that the underprivilaged "will envy the favored ones their privileges and will do all they can to free themselves from their own surplus of privation."[5]

In <u>The Moving Target</u> class tension, and its racial corollary, is made manifest when Attorney

_____

[2]Sigmund Freud, <u>Civilization and its Discontents</u> trans. James Strachey (New York: W.W. Norton & Co., 1961), p. 58.

[3]<u>Ibid.</u>, p. 62.

[4]<u>Ibid.</u>, p. 23.

[5]Freud, <u>Future of an Illusion</u>, p. 12.

Abbert Graves questions the servants about the ransom note. Felix, the Sampson's Filipino houseboy, tells Archer, "I resent Mr. Graves' assumption that I am suspect because of the color of my skin. The gardeners also resent it for themselves."[6] But Graves also suffers the pains of social distinction. Though moderately successful, the contrast between Graves' life and that of his wealthy clients constantly reveals the renunciations that his life demands. Once a respected district attorney and possible political candidate, he has given up public service to accept the retainers of the wealthy. When he enters the tale he is pretending to pay attention to a rich old woman who is "telling him how clever he was, very clever and helpful."[7] Graves' resentments over the renunciations demanded of him are heightened by the fact that he sees daily the rewards that others receive, and these resentments ultimately lead him to commit murder in an attempt to satisfy the sexual and ambitious wishes that are denied him. And the renunciations of Sampson's pilot, Alan Taggart, are even greater.

Society pays a steep price in unhappiness and discord for social inequality. One might expect that Freud would be an advocate of socialist reform as the path to an ideal society. But Freud believes that "the inclination to aggression is an original, self-subsisting instinctual disposition"[8] which, ought to be controlled and channeled but which cannot be destroyed. Property is simply a socially acceptable means of expressing aggression and social difference.

The Moving Target[9] explores the way in which

---

[6]The Moving Target,. p. 129.

[7]Ibid., p. 13.

[8]Freud, Civilization and its Discontents, p. 69.

[9]In the first Lew Archer novel, The Moving Target, Archer is hired to look for kidnapped oil millionaire, Ralph Sampson. Before the end of the novel, Sampson himself is implicated in a crime, a variety of villains emerge, and two

20

the struggle over property brings about socially unacceptable expressions of aggression as well. Millionaire Ralph Sampson has been kidnapped and Archer must look for clues in the personal and social tensions which led most Sampson's family and associates to despise him. For both youthful Alan Taggert and the middle-aged Albert Graves the assertion of self is finally expressed in a grasping at property in which their ambitious desires are complicated by their connection to erotic wishes. Both men come to believe that their erotic and ambitious satisfactions are connected and are to be achieved by seizing the property (and in Graves' case the daughter) of Ralph Sampson.

A Shared Fantasy Life

With the publication of <u>Totem and Taboo</u> in 1913, Freud asserts "the existence of a collective mind, in which mental processes occur just as they do in the mind of the individual."[10] If the analogy is accurate, then the "collective mind" ought to have its fantasies, just as the individual mind does. And in "Creative Writers and Day-Dreaming" Freud examines the popular culture of his day as a shared fantasy life analogous to the day dreaming of individuals. Approached in this way the tale reveals the unconscious concerns of the collective mind. Freud's work seems to support a case for a societal unconscious that is rooted in a basic human psychology but which, unlike what Carl Jung called the collective unconscious, remains culturally specific. Though

---

likeable characters prove willing to commit murder in order to take from Sampson the resources to satisfy their erotic and ambitious desires. As the story progresses, Archer's task expands so that in addition to recovering Ralph Sampson, he seeks to assist Sampson's daughter Miranda in the process of individuation.

[10]Sigmund Freud, <u>Totem and Taboo</u>, trans. James Strachey (New York: W.W. Norton & Co., 1950), p. 157.

the model is not without its faults[11] it does present some unique advantages even at the point where it is rightly criticized. A Freudian conception of human development which gives play to the unconscious (as a social learning model does not) accounts for much about the way our sexual selves are embedded in the unconscious and given expression in society. Freud recognizes that gender is fundamental to our identity and the stress he lays on the importance of fantasy in working out our identity within society underlies the present work.

The metaphor of dreaming has often led Freudian criticism toward literary biography with the text being regarded as the dream-like expression of the author's unconscious. Certainly Ross Macdonald's work can be read in this way. But our interest is with the Macdonald texts as examples of popular culture and a psychoanalytic reading should aid in our consideration of the way the tales manifest the unconscious concerns of the audience rather than the author.

2) Freud's Analysis of Popular Culture

Remembering that Freud's own models for describing the personality were narratives such as the tale of Oedipus, it should not suprise us that we can identify Freudian patterns within popular novels and films. The important question is whether identifying these patterns helps to relate the tale to the psychological and social forces at work upon the audience.

While we think of critical analysis of popular culture as a relatively recent phenomenon, Freud himself was interested in the application of his

---

[11]Freud's model of human develpment treats male sexuality as normative and much of his discussion of women reflects the patriarchy of his day. As with any methodology one must be sensitive to the degree to which the appraoch is bound by the society within which it was created, as is much of Freud's discussion of women and their sexuality. But the benefits of a psychological approach which is rooted in an understanding of society continues to make Freud useful.

theories to the work of "less pretentious authors of novels, romances and short stories, who nevertheless have the widest and most eager circle of readers of both sexes[12] In the essay, "Creative Writers and Day-dreaming," Freud attempts an explanation of the popularity of mass market entertainments.

The work of the writer at first seems unlike anything which other people do. However, Freud' suggests it is analogous to the activity of children at play in that the writer "creates a world of his own, or rather rearranges the things of his world in a new way which pleases him."[13] The child who plays at being a parent, a firefighter, or some other adult persona desires the powers and freedoms which adults appear to have and therefore enters into a fantasy in which this wish is fulfilled. The psychological purpose of this imaginative play is to provide the illusion of mastery over a world in which the child is relatively powerless. Elsewhere, Freud writes,

> It is clear that in their play children repeat everything that has made a great impression on them in real life, and that in doing so they abreact ["abreaction" is the expression or release of previously repressed emotions.] the strength of the impression and, as one might put it, make themselves master of the situation.[14]

The child knows that the fantasy is not "real" but nonethe-less treats it with the utmost seriousness. Play is both a part of the child's effort to understand the world and an expression of his or her desire to control that world.

Gradually, in growing up, one comes to feel shame about the public enactment of these wishes and ceases to play. If adult life actually

---

12Freud, "Creative Writers and Day-dreaming," p. 149.

13Ibid., pp. 143-44.

14Sigmund Freud, Beyond the Pleasure Principle, trans. James Strachey (New York: W.W. Norton & Co., 1961), p. 11.

23

provides the unlimited powers and freedoms which the child perceives, this would be quite understandable; but it does not. Though the frustration of our desires may vary by the nature and social situation of the individual, we all lack the powers and freedoms which as children we imagined adults possessed and thus each of us has unfulfilled wishes. Freud tells us that "these motivating wishes . . . are either ambitious wishes, which serve to elevate the subject's personality; or they are erotic ones.[15] Unable to renounce the pleasure of play, most people replace the outwardly expressed play with daydreams that serve the same end. Thus our dissatisfactions with our actual situation are, at least temporarily, satisfied by daydreams in which we fantasize ourselves as heroes.

However, this substitution of the adolescent or adult daydream for the play of the child presents a problem for the fantisizer. As children we shared our play and did not hide it from others. But as adults we conceal this activity and discover that we find no pleasure in anothers fantasy. The obvious connection between the hero of the fantasy and ego of the fantasizer prevent us from entering anothers fantasy and sharing in its satisfactions.

Popular culture provides public fantasies which may be shared and discussed like the play which we knew as children. These public fantasies are expressed through stories which are re-fashionings of familiar material from "the popular treasure-house of myths, legends, and fairy tales," and they are probably "distorted vestiges of the wishful phantasies of whole nations, the secular dreams of youthful humanity."[16] What set the popular story apart from other daydreams is the writer's ability to disguise the connection between the hero and the author/day-dreamer while providing aesthetic satisfactions in the presentation of the fantasy so that any number of people may take pleasure in the fantasy.[17] The

---

[15]Ibid., pp. 146-47.

[16]Ibid., p. 152.

[17]Ibid., see p.153.

popular text, or more narrowly, the fantasy behind it, then belongs to the audience, that is to society. Just as the individual's dreams are interpreted by the analyst as transformations of the personal anxieties and wishes of the dreamer, the popular story gives us a glimpse of the transformed wishes and anxieties of an audience.

In order to enter into the public fantasies of popular culture rather than the private fantasy of his or her own creation, the audience member gives up the overt relationship of his or her ego with the hero. But this pleasure is in fact only disguised, for the fantasizer may, in reading or in subsequent reflection, in fact replace the hero with his or her own ego. In return for this additional step, the consumer is rewarded with a fantasy which may be publicly enjoyed and shared with others - since he or she may easily deny the connection between the hero and the ego. Freud offers us a psychological explanation of the sociological function of popular culture. This shared fantasy has the possibility of integrating the fantasizer into society, whereas the shame inherent in the private day dream alienates the fantasizer.

If Freud is right about the source of the appeal of popular culture, then there must exist shared dissatisfactions within the audience which the fantasy temporarily satisfies. A study of popular culture will thus reveal unhappinesses within the culture and point to the devices by which the society protects itself against those dissatisfactions. This transformation of basic dissatisfactions by means of fantasy is an unconscious process that occurs in both the individual and the group. For the group, as with individuals, the fantasy which pleases may be either healthy or unhealthy. Psychoanalytic literary critic Norman Holland argues, "There is no guarantee that a plot - or any transformational device in literature - moves in the direction of maturation."[18] If we are to use this ideal as a critical model for the study of popular culture, we will then ask of the popular story: with whom will the audience identify in this tale, what is the unfulfilled wish which is

---

[18]Norman N. Holland, The Dynamics of Literary Response (New York: W.W. Norton & Comp., 1975), p. 105.

given expression here, and what are the implications
of that adaptation to the dynamics of life in society?

Wish Fulfillment and The Moving Target

In "Creative Writing and Day-Dreaming" Freud
focuses on the hero to the exclusion of other characters
in considering with whom the readers will identify.
It may be that this is not always the case. Some
readers may at times identify with other characters
of their own sex or race. One must proceed with
caution in asserting that we know how any particular
reader uses the tale. But given this caution it
seems reasonable to assume that most readers, most
of the time, identify with the protaganist and are
drawn to genres in which this identification is
relatively easy for them. Thus, in considering
Macdonald's fiction we will assume that it is Lew
Archer with whom the audience identifies and
consider what sort of wishes are satisfied by such
an identification.

As with any popular genre, hard-boiled detective
fiction includes tales that offer different degrees
of wish fulfillment. For instance, in considering
the espionage novels of Ian Fleming, one turns readily
to the simplest sort of wish fulfillment to explain
the popularity of the dashing James Bond. But the
same genre encompasses John Le Carre's fat, cuckolded,
spy, George Smiley. And, similarly, within the hard-
boiled genre John D. MacDonald's sybaritic hero,
Travis McGee, is a more obvious candidate for wish
fulfillment analysis than Dashiell Hammett's Continental
Op. When we turn our attention to the wishes fulfilled
by the genre stories of Le Carre, Hammett, and Ross
Macdonald, we come to understand why Freud included
mightmares within the continuum of wish fulfillment.

A glance at the jackets of any rack of paperback
mysteries suggest that erotic fantasy plays a role
in the marketing of the genre and certainly hardboiled
detective fiction has its share of sex. The ethical
concern credited to Hammett's Sam Spade in Chapter
One didn't prevent Spade's affair with his partner's
wife (which preceded the novel) or his involvement
with his client. But there is a tension in the genre
which often undercuts the fulfillment of erotic wishes.
The genre's focus on responsibility, which will be
discussed more fully in the next chapter, seems to
place limits on the protaganist's libido. And Ross

26

Macdonald's Lew Archer seems the most restrained detective of the genre.

Of the women with whom Archer deals in The Moving Target, young and attractive Miranda Sampson seems the most likely object of erotic fantasy. Certainly she is such an object for Albert Graves, whom Archer describes as "at forty . . . drunk on love."[19] In a curious triangle she is obviously infatuated with Sampson's pilot, Alan Taggart, who seems only bemused by her interest. There is a sexual tension between Archer and Miranda evident in her effort to use a flirtation with the detective to arouse Taggart, but it remains repressed behind Archer's sense of responsibility for her so that he says, "My obscure resentment came out as fatherly advice."[20]

One evidence of the accuracy of Freud's suggestion that wish fulfilment is a primary function of popular culture lies in translating Macdonald for the screen. In both the film based upon The Drowning Pool and the made-for-TV movie based on The Underground Man, the female clients are transformed into former lovers of the detective.

The film maker's tendency to move toward the most direct forms of wish fulfillment is also evident in Harper, the film based on The Moving Target, though it has a different expression. In the novel Archer is put off balance by Miranda's flirtation, and his fatherly response, which draws attention to the Oedipal tensions, seems to provide him with protection from the sexual appeal of the young woman. As portrayed by Paul Newman, the detective has a distance and self assurance that lessens the tension because he seems more clearly in control of the situation.

The film also provides an alternative, and potentially more acceptable, subject for Archer's attentions. The detective's divorce from Susan, which in the novel lies somewhere in Archer's past, is brought into the present. This allows a series of comic contacts by phone in which the detective

---

[19]Macdonald, The Moving Target, (New York: Bantam, 1970), p. 15.

[20]Ibid., p. 84.

attempts to maintain control of the marital relationship, and a final night of (off screen) intercourse which ironically serves to prove that Susan is right in her assumption that he can never give himself as fully to marriage as he does to the short-term commitments of his work. There may be a degree of wish-fulfillment in Macdonald's presentation of a life free of marital responsibility, but contrasted with more traditional wish-fulfillment figures it would seem that the fulfillment of sexual wishes plays a minimal part in the appeal of Macdonald's novels.

It may be ambitious, rather than sexual, wishes which are fulfilled by the Archer novels. In the classical tradition of the detective story it was common to have a hero who enjoyed the rewards of superior intelligence, social position, or both. Consider the various English gentlemen detectives, such as Dorothy Sayers' Lord Peter Wimsey, who were often defered to by the police or the upper class American detectives in the classical tradition such as the brilliant and well-to-do Nero Wolfe, or Hammett's witty socialites Nick and Nora Charles. The reader who identifies with characters such as these, with their possessions and position, may easily be thought to be fulfilling ambitious wishes.

But what is the attraction of the lowly working detective of the hard-boiled tradition? Here is a usually middle-aged loner struggling to maintain a lower middle class life style, one who lives in rented rooms, who is often persecuted by the authorities. There are exceptions to the norm, such as Robert B. Parker's gourmet detective, Spencer, but Macdonald's Lew Archer is not atypical of the genre.

In spite of Archer's lack of the most common trappings of ambitious wishes - status, wealth, and authority - a study of The Moving Target suggests that the genre does offer an oblique satisfaction of the reader's ambitious wishes. While we never have our wishes gratified by the obvious devices of the having the detective achieve wealth or social success, the tale provides alternative satisfactions for these wishes through questioning such values in secondary characters, by contrasting their lives with that of the protaganist, and by inviting the reader to renounce as unsatisfactory such id-inspired desires.

The tale challenges the economic transposition of the id. Macdonald seems to suggest that great wealth offers no real satisfactions to those who have it and indeed seems responsible for how shallow their lives are. Wealth makes slaves of those who strive after it and undercuts their ethical standards. Their striving typically leads to prison or death. It is the Sampsons, with their seaside mansion, servants, private plane, and swimming pool, who represent the moneyed classes in The Moving Target. They have everything that money can buy, but are presented as neurotic, unhappy, manipulative, insincere, and childish. Sampson's money, rather than improving the family's situation, ultimately costs him his life.

Within the tale it is Albert Graves who, like Freud's ambitious wisher, longs to be one of the Sampsons. The desire for material success has taken him out of the District Attorney's office and into private practice, and his ambitious and erotic wishes combine in his infatuation with Miranda Sampson. His desires keep Graves in bondage to the Sampsons while his frustrations make him appear to be a fool and ultimately lead to murder.

This trusted professional and family confident presents the greatest challenge to Archer's ego control of the tale. Though Graves' romantic and sexual infatuation with Miranda seems mostly to bemuse the detective, it prepares us for his connected but greater failings. His actions prove to be a betrayal of Archer and the things for which the detective stands.

The other figures whose wishes lead them to aspire after what the Sampsons have are the kidnappers, the villians of the tale, who are driven by a naive hope for a romantic escape funded by Sampson's wealth. Their plotting leads to their deaths.

Authority is an alternative to wealth as a satisfaction of ambitious wishes. The police are the usual representatives of civil authority in the detective story. But just as Macdonald suggest that the satisfaction of the fantasy of possessing wealth is an unsatisfactory path to happiness, the fantasy of having authority is also ultimately unfulfilling. Often, the police in the genre, as in Chandler's Bay City, are presented as corrupt. At other times, as with Sheriff Spanner and his half-witted deputy in <u>The Moving Target</u>, they are incompetent.

It was suggested in Chapter One that the fictional private detective is often a former police officer, that is, one who has had authority, seen its limits, and given it up. So it is with Archer. In <u>The Moving Target</u>, where Archer is called into the case because Albert Graves knows him from the days when Archer was an employee of the District Attorney's office.

Over against the dark picture of success that is painted in <u>The Moving Target</u>, and indeed throughout the genre, the life of the detective is offered. When wealth and authority are presented as unable to deliver satisfaction, then the better way is to renounce these false satisfactions. Possessing neither wealth nor authority, Lew Archer is his own person, and since the tale is told in his voice, we see the wealthy and those in authority as he does. Where others are servants to wealth or authority, he has an independence that grows out of his refusal to make the compromises which other characters make. While the failure of Archer's marriage makes it clear that there is a price for this independence, the detective demonstrates a moral superiority over others in his tale.

As with the films based on <u>The Drowning Pool</u> and <u>The Underground Man</u>, there is a tendency in translating such tales for the broader audiences of television and film to alter them in order to offer more traditional erotic and ambitious satisfactions. The intellectualized displacement of the traditional fantasy satisfactions is a limited pleasure with a relatively narrow audience. The audience for Macdonald and writers like him shares the dissatisfactions of their society but they distance themselves from the larger audience of more popular hard-boiled fiction by their acceptance of a double displacement from the common unhappiness.

When popular texts are regarded as "the wishful phantasies of whole nations"[21] then the importance of their analysis for the student of contemporary culture is obvious. We are here developing a

---

[21]Freud, "Creative Writers and Day-Dreaming," p. 152.

method of identifying the wishes of a culture and of particular groups within a culture. These wishes in turn reveal the desires and dissatisfactions of the group and the method thus becomes a valuable tool for the exploration of cultural conflict and consensus about attitudes, values, and aspirations.

Some Problems with the Wish Fulfillment Theory

If we do not overly simplify the concept, it is hard to think of an example of popular culture that does not reflect some degree of wish fulfillment. But several nagging problems present themselves in carrying out such an analysis. First of all, we know that writers as central to genre as Raymond Chandler have argued that they were in fact realists. Secondly, for all the tendency toward wish fulfillment that has been demonstrated within the genre, the protagonists demonstrate a high degree of renunciation (of erotic and ambitious wishes) and a moralism which seems at odds with this tendency.

Chandler's "realism" can, as was argued in Chapter One, be taken with a grain of salt. He uses the term to refer to a particular attitude toward the world and to the social class of his hero. Certainly his work is as romantic as that of the classical detective writers which he and others of the "Black Mask" school reacted against. But we should not flee too quickly from the claim, for it explains in part the second problem in applying the wish fulfillment theory, i.e., the level of renunciation of the hero in some hard-boiled tales.

Wish fulfillment seems to be a primary human satisfaction which can serve society both by preserving the status quo and by encouraging development. First, wish fulfillment is a conservative force in society that offers fantasy satisfactions for unhappinesses which might disrupt society if they were not limited in this way.[22] Secondly, where a fiction like

---

[22]Obviously where the society being studied is seen as essentially just, the analyst will value this adjustment to unavoidable dissatisfaction. Where the repressions demanded by a society are unjust this displacement of satisfaction into fantasy may be seen as a repressive force which resists social change.

Macdonald's encourages renunciation as a path to ultimately higher satisfactions, it becomes a progressive force for the advancement of society. It is true that the translation of hard-boiled novels for film or television, with the attendant need to attract a larger portion of the mass audience, has tended to decrease the degree of renunciation and increase the hero's action out of wishes. But the idea of wish fulfillment does not present an exhaustive psychoanalytic description of the function of popular culture within a society anymore than it provides a full description of the function of dreaming for the individual. Clearly the work of both the collective and individual unconscious should not be reduced to this single function. There are other psychological satisfactions which the popular arts provide. Holland,[23] for example, suggests that in addition to wish fulfillment, fantasies may serve the purpose of anxiety mastery. This helps us to see that one might take satisfaction either in identifying with a hero who expresses ego desires which we share or with a hero who successfully faces renunciations or social restraints which we also share.

3) Narrative Analysis

Let us consider what the narrative, read as a psychoanalyst might read a personality, suggests about the forces at play within The Moving Target and what they suggest about the world view of the audience. Though Freud saw himself as a scientist, he can be seen as offering a hermeneutic, a canon of interpretation of human experience. For instance, the conflicts that psychoanalysis describes in the personality can readily be found within the hard-boiled narrative.[24]

---

[23]Dynamics of Literary Response, see p. 32.

[24]This approach to textual description and interpretation was used in "A Freudian Analysis of the Private Detective Tale," Stuart M. Kaminsky with Jeffrey H. Mahan, American Television Genres (Chicago: Nelson-Hall, 1985) p. 145ff.

The unconscious life of an individual is shaped by powerful forces that Freud called id, ego, and superego. One source of the gratification that a story provides seems to be the examination in fantasy of the conflicts between these forces.

One way to examine the characters within a story is by noting which unconscious force is predominant in shaping their actions. At times this can be done simply as by assigning the role of id, ego, or superego to a character. The hero can often be equated with the ego, while the id and superego are represented by other characters, as though these forces were actual willful beings. In this way we arrive at a model for describing narrative conflict that may explain why conflict seems necessary to the audience's satisfaction with a tale. This reductionist model runs the risk of oversimplifying and thus distorting a more complicated narrative. But the conflict between id, ego, and superego remains a useful approach to narrative description if we recognize that most characters, like most people, are subject to shifts in the way they are affected by these forces. The protagonist usually represents the ego's control of the conflicting pressures of the id and superego whose powers in turn are represented by other characters, as though these forces were actual willful beings. In this way we arrive at a model for describing narrative conflict that may explain why conflict seems necessary to the audience's satisfaction with a tale.

Within the unconscious the id reflects the universal concern for self-gratification. The id's desires are unbound by any recognition of the limitations imposed by nature, our bodies, or society. The id desires all things, is unable to delay gratifications, and is unrestrained by the constraints of reality. Freud tells us that "the logical laws of thought do not apply in the id, impulses exist side by side, without canceling each other out or diminishing each other."[25] The id

---

[25]Sigmund Freud, New Introductory Lecture on Psychoanalysis, trans. James Strachey (New York: W.W. Norton & Co., 1964), p. 65.

simultaneously wants every pleasure, even those that are in conflict with each other, such as autonomy and community.

According to Freud, we begin life totally subject to the irrational demands of the id. But we cannot remain in such a state. The ego is the mechanism of social balance that represents the external world to the id.[26] As our perceptual systems develop, we come to relate cause and effect, and the ego grows and is strengthened. The ego is the rational and reasonable portion of the unconscious which struggles to organize and satisfy the demands of the id. Gradually the ego takes over much of the authority of the id. But the ego never fully frees itself from the demands of the id. The ego has no energy of its own and is fueled by the id's strivings.

There is another force within the unconscious bearing down upon the ego which Freud calls the superego. The superego is an internalized moral authority related to the idea of conscience which grows out of the social restraint imposed by family and society. Like the ego, the superego developes in childhood. Free of the constraints of the superego, the very young child obeys only when the parental authority is present. But just as each of us must develop an ego, we must develop a superego.

Using a male model, Freud traces this development in his discussion of the Oedipal crisis. The mother is the main source of pleasure for a young boy and so he wishes to possess her. Ruled by the id, the boy wishes to destroy the immensely powerful rival for her attention and affection, his father. At the same time, his ego realizes the power of the father and fears him. The child's response to these conflicting emotions is to internalize the father and to identify with him and his power. This identification brings forth the internalized authority figure called the super-ego. Though based on external authorities, the superego is a harsh and punitive parody of them which "applies the strictest moral standard to the helpless ego."[27] Unlike the child's

---

[26]Ibid., See especially, p. 67.

[27]Ibid., p. 54.

parent or teacher, the superego is constantly present and punishes, not only the actual transgression, but the desire to transgress as well. The superego's power to punish the desire as well as the act creates a conflict with the ego which we experience as guilt.

In addition to the id and superego, there is a third pressure upon the ego which we have not yet discussed, that of external reality. The forces of nature, the limitations of the body, and the restrictions of society all place constraints on the individual with which the ego must contend. Thus the rational center of the self, the ego, must constantly balance three powerful forces: id, superego, and external reality.

When the ego fails, or comes near to failing, to balance the three forces, anxiety is produced. Pressure from the superego produces moral anxiety. Pressure from the id produces anxiety about our powers and possessions. Pressure from the external world produces what can be called realistic anxiety.

The ego develops a variety of defense mechanisms to protect us from anxiety. These defenses may produce fantasies that deny or alter reality in order to allow the ego to cope with internal needs. At other times, the ego may identify with the threatening force or displace anxiety so that our feelings are acted out, not on the forbidden object, but on some other, less protected object.

The goal of psychoanalysis is first to understand the forces that bear upon the individual's ego and then to strengthen the ego so that it can better balance those pressures. Though the id and superego seem opposite forces within the unconscious, the well-developed individual will make little use of the superego, because the strengthened ego is strong enough to control the id rationally.

When we bring these insights about the individual unconscious to bear upon cultural fantasies, they reveal the tale's unconscious structures. Freud's assertion of a "collective mind"[28] in combination with his discussion of popular culture lead one to suggest that such material reflects a societal uncon-

---

[28]Freud, _Totem and Taboo_, p. 157.

sious. If this is so, the answer to the tale's popularity lies in part in its ability to represent and resolve the struggle for psychic balance that we all share.

While all people share the same basic struggle for psychic balance, different cultures and different audiences within a culture face different pressures and accept different solutions to the demands placed upon the ego. A critical approach to popular culture informed by Freud's psychoanalytic approach to the personality should increase our understanding of the universal tensions and anxieties expressed in the text and of the unique expression of those tensions within a particular societal unconscious. From this we come to understand the satisfactions that the tale offers to a particular audience.

Ego Structures in The Moving Target

The first-person protagonist, Lew Archer, more than any other character, represents balanced ego control in Macdonald's work. With each encounter the detective forces other characters, dominated in various ways by the id or superego, to confront their own imbalances. Here Freud's model of the individual is appropriated as a social model which reveals the "sick" society or sub-culture that Macdonald portrays and that the ego urges toward mental health.

The novels begin with the ego figure (Archer) at rest and quickly bring some challenge or temptation to bear upon the ego's control of the situation. The detective's function as ego is to evaluate and balance these pressures that come to bear upon him and thus to restore ego balance to the social situation examined in the tale. Archer describes this evaluative responsibility, which he calls "judging," during his drive with Miranda to the Temple in the Clouds. Their conversation (in Chapter 15) comes roughly in the middle of the thirty-one chapter novel and allows for philosophical reflection on the meaning of the case. Archer says of himself and his work:

'I used to think the world was divided into good people and bad people, and that you could pin responsibility for evil on certain definite people and punish the guilty. I'm still going through the motions . . . most of my work is watching people, and judging them.'[29]

Watching and before judging, evaluating the forces that come to bear upon it, are the tasks of the ego. And Archer has discovered that he must make judgments which are at once more complex and more pragmatic than the crude judging of the superego.

In the detective story, the client makes id-like demands upon the detective. And just as the ego draws its energy from the demand of the id, the detective is impowered by the client. The Moving Target begins with Archer summoned by Sampson's invalid wife, Elaine, to the Sampson's Cabrillo Canyon estate.[30] The id's demands are evident in her desire to have the detective at her beck and call, her unhappiness at his inability to be simultaneously in attendance and out working on the case, and in her open expression of her desire to survive her husband and inherit his wealth. Archer seems to feel a primarily professional obligation to her. It is in his relationship to her step-daughter, Miranda, that we see something approaching the detective's conventional concern for the well being of the client. Archer attempts to move Miranda away from an id-dominated state to balanced ego control of her life. This is accomplished as they search for her troubled and troubling and quite repressed superego, Ralph Sampson.

Archer is hired to search for Ralph Sampson. But, as the tale progresses, Sampson is portrayed less and less sympathetically until one wonders whether anyone really wants to see his return. Mrs. Sampson says that, sober, her husband is "half man, half alligator, half bear trap," When he is drinking Sampson looks for a surrogate parent "to blow his nose and dry away his tears and spank him when he's naughty." She continues: "Do I sound

---

[29]Ross Macdonald, The Moving Target, p. 82.

[30]As with General Sternwood in Chandler's The Big Sleep, Sampsons's wealth and position make it possible to send for the detective rather than visiting his office as would most clients.

cruel? I'm just being objective."[31] Archer warns
against the company Sampson has been keeping, "bad
as there is in Los Angeles, and that's as bad as
there is."[32] Even Sampson's daughter, Miranda,
eventually admits that "he's always been a bit of a
stinker."[33]

Sampson seems to serve as the repository of
the repressions of all the other characters. In
fact, with the kidnapping he is literally repressed.
Sampson is at once the possessor of all of the things
that others in the tale wish for but lack, and the
harsh judging authority whom they cannot satisfy.
Thus their ambivalence about whether they want him
released or not becomes understandable. In order
to solve the case, Archer must analyze what Sampson's
wife, daughter, employees, and friends have projected
on the kidnapped oil millionaire.

It is Archer's freedom from Sampson's psychological
and financial power which frees him to move the tale
toward an ego-balanced resolution. Already kidnapped
when Archer comes into the case and dead when Archer
finds him, Sampson exerts none of his judgmental
authority upon the detective.

Outside the circle of the Sampsons' friends
and trusted employees stand Dwight Troy and his cohorts,
Fay Estabrook and Claude, who represent the active
domination of the id within The Moving Target and
whom Archer seems unable to change or convert. Ralph
Sampson works with Troy and Claude to bring in undocumented workers from Mexico and this conspiracy
expresses the moral connection between Sampson and
the gangster who shares his lack of ego balance.
Dwight Troy makes minimal effort to disguise his
commitment to self-interest. As we see more of
him, it becomes clear that he resists all restraints
upon his desires. Archer is told by the authorities
that Troy has been involved in bootlegging and
gambling, always moving on when "his protection

---

[31]Macdonald, The Moving Target, pp. 4,5.

[32]Ibid., p. 69.

[33]Ibid., p. 83.

wears thin."[34]   Troy and his assistants are powerful representatives of the id who actively resist Archer's attempt to gain ego control of the tale.

But throughout much of the novel the representative of the id, on which the conflict in the tale turns, remains hidden. In the mystery story the id must not only be resisted, but first discovered, revealed, and faced by the ego. So it often is in the unconscious. The id disguises itself, makes itself appealing. Archer says, when he discovers that Sampson's pilot, Alan Taggers, is responsible for unleashing the events of the tale, "I'd have seen it sooner if I hadn't happened to like you."[35]

It is Taggert, in league with his lover, Betty Fraley, who is the true antagonist. The self-serving power of the id is fully evident in Taggert's readiness to kill Archer, in order to guarantee his "freedom of action."[36] Once released, the id is difficult to constrain. The ego's struggle within the narrative reveals and disrupts the subsidiary id figures: Sampson, Troy, and Graves. Sampson's character is exposed and ultimately his life is forfeited; Troy's current racket is upset; and Graves makes an irreversible submission to the temptations of the id.

Archer's old friend, Sampson's attorney, Albert Graves, is the saddest of the id's representatives. Graves is a good man gone bad. His years among the wealthy have infected him with the striving of the id. The current District Attorney says of him that his lifetime of striving failed to make him the equal of his wealthy clients "the whole thing suddenly went sour. . . . There was no more virtue or justice, in him or in the world.'[37] For years he has successfully restrained his desires and channeled

---

[34]Ibid., p. 65.

[35]Ibid., p. 137.

[36]Ibid., p. 139.

[37]Ibid., p. 184.

them through his move out of public service and into a private law practice. But his dissatisfactions surface in his foolish infatuation with Miranda Sampson. Finally he strikes out and kills the uncouth man who has all the things he has come to want. In a bizarre Oedipal triangle, Albert Graves, who is old enough to be her father, kills Miranda Sampson's father in order to possess the young woman and the money and power she inherits. Archer tells us, "Crime is like that, . . . it's epidemic."[38]

The Forces of the Superego

Though the forces of the id seem to predominate in The Moving Target, our model suggests that we consider also the other two forces, the superego and external reality, which come to bear upon the ego. But how are the pressures of the superego to be distinguished from those of external reality? In the psychoanalysis of an individual the problem is simpler, for the superego lies within the unconscious of the individual. In applying these concepts to a narrative we must distinguish those characters who represent the superego's harsh judgment and readiness to punish from those who represent the realistic limitations of the world.

The distinction is clarified if we remember that Freud did not oppose the parental authority that produced the superego. Indeed he regarded the parent who combined judgment with affection as necessary for the individual's safe growth and integration into society. Similarly, not all societal authority is to be disapproved of; the id must be constrained. What Freud attempted to overcome through psychoanalysis was superego's irrational expression of judgment cut off from a legitimate concern for the self. The goal of ego psychology is to replace the irrational repression of the id with its rational control by the ego.

Such a distinction clarifies the differences in Archer's relationship to a range of characters who are the official representatives of the authority of the state. The hard-boiled detective's independence

---

[38]Ibid., p. 183.

always makes for a difficult relationship with the police. But there are distinctions to be made between "good cops" and "bad cops" based on their integrity, competence, and use of the authority inherent in their roles. In The Moving Target, Sheriff Spanner and his deputy represent the superego by their harsh and inappropriate use of a judgmental authority.

The local sheriff is portrayed as both incompetent and officious. Suggesting that th D.A.'s fingerprint expert is better qualified than the sheriff's,[39] Albert Graves invites Humphreys (Graves' successor as District Attorney) to become personally involved. The comparative competence of the sheriff and the current District Attorney is reflected in their staffs. The sheriff's first representative on the scene is a deputy so incompetent that he has to be told by Archer not to handle the ransom note until it has been fingerprinted.[40]

It is not their incompetence that aligns the sheriff and his deputy with the superego. Rather their incompetence reveals a deeper failing, the irrationality and lack of social utility of their expressions of power. They enact authority for its own sake and thus are figures of repression. Archer says of the sheriff when he first arrives that "like his clothes, his face was hybrid, half cop and half politician."[41] The suggestion of compromise in that description reveals the uncompromising detective's attitude toward the sheriff who, as Archer feared, assumes that authority will resolve the situation. He has to be told "in words of one syllable"[42] that if he arrests the person who picks up the ransom he further endangers Ralph Sampson.

Freud tells us that the well developed ego has little use for the superego. The ego seeks to use

---

[39]Ibid., p. 94.

[40]Ibid., p. 94.

[41]Ibid., p. 100.

[42]Ibid.

41

reason rather than authority to overcome the id.
So it is with Archer, who resists the encroachment
of the superego, often using insult and, especiall
in the later novels, irony as his weapons.

We see this struggle when Archer refuses to
be frisked by the sheriff's moronic deputy. Aloofly
superior, he insults the deputy both in ways he understands and in ways which are over his head. But,
places his goals above his attitude about the
incompetent police man he finally forces himself to
acknowledge the man's authority, finally calling
him "officer."[43] Both the writer and the detective
are less mature than they will be in subsequent
novels and the struggle with the superego is
difficult for both. Macdonald creates a stereotypical
dumb cop and Archer directly challenges his
authority. But even here, when Archer manages to
get out the word "officer," there is a recognition
that this conflict with unreasonable authority must
itself be constrained by reason.

Archer again asserts his independence from the
super ego's demands when challenges by Sheriff Spanner
to account for his actions:

> 'You were looking for Sampson,' he said,
> with heavy irony. 'You expect me to take your
> word for that.'
> 'You don't have to take my word. I'm not
> working for you.'
> He leaned toward me with his hands on his
> hips. 'If I wanted to be ugly, I could put
> you away this minute.'
> My patience broke. 'Don't look now,' I said,
> 'but you are ugly.'
> 'Do you know who you're talking to?'
> 'A sheriff. A sheriff with a tough case
> on his hands, and no ideas. So you're looking
> for a goat.'[44]

It is not unreasonable for the police to want to
know about the activities of those connected with
the case. What Archer resists is not the desire

---

[43]Ibid., see the incident, pp. 110-11.

[44]Ibid., p. 147.

to be informed but the insistence that control of the case be decided on the basis of arbitrary authority rather than a rational consideration of experience and competence. Having stood up for his own independence, Archer goes on to tell the sheriff about Dwight Troy's alien smuggling racket. This shared confidence at once makes the detective seem to cooperate and refocuses the sheriff's attentions, leaving Archer free to proceed with his investigation of the Sampson kidnapping.

There is another figure in the tale who attempts to assert the power of the superego. Claude, the keeper of the Temple in the Clouds, claims the authority of a priest in ordering Archer and Miranda away. "You must not enter the temple. It would anger Mithras."[45] And when it is clear that they will not be deterred, "The sacrilege will rest upon your heads."[46]

There is little sign of traditional religious authority within Archer's world. Whether the names of the gods are evoked sincerely, as when, in The Underground Man, Mrs. Broadhurst calls her late father "a god come down to earth in human guise"[47] or by a charlatan like The Moving Target's Claude, Macdonald tends to use it as a sign of unbalance, of the surrender to a harsh and alien authority. We are told that Ralph Sampson accepts Claude as a genuine religious figure, but this is undercut by the discovery that the undocumented workers staying at the temple are enroute to Sampson's ranch. However seriously Sampson takes the sun-worship, his apparently genuine interest in astrology represents a similar surrender to irrational spiritual authority.

---

[45]Ibid., p. 87.

[46]Ibid.

[47]Ross Macdonald, The Underground Man (New York: Bantam Books, 1972), p. 132.

43

The Forces of External Reality

One of the tasks of the ego is to enable the individual to accept the limits of external reality. Our humanness, the powers of nature, and the limitations imposed by society must be accepted by the individual who is to live successfully in the world. The world which Macdonald creates also has limits imposed by its creator, and Archer is distinguished from those dominated by the id and superego by his recognition of the limits imposed by that reality.

When Taggert (a figure dominated by the id) is ready to kill him, Archer attempts to make the kidnapper see the way that external reality will impinge on the action. "Shooting me . . . It'll guarantee . . . death by gas."[48] Throughout the novel, Archer makes Albert Graves self conscious about his infatuation with Miranda Sampson. The detective's very presence seems to make the middle-aged attorney aware of how unlikely a successful marriage is with the wealthy young beauty. Similarly, faced with battling the powerful ex-boxer, Puddler, Archer recognizes his own physical limitations.

In Macdonald's world there will always be a tension between the independent private detective and the public detectives. However the detective respect for some police officers suggests that it is possible for them to be the representatives of the appropriate limits of society. Humphreys, the local district attorney, and Peter Colton, Archer's contact in the Los Angeles district attorney's office, are authority figures who represent the legitimate restraining influence of society respected by the ego.

In a visit important enough to be given its own chapter Archer turns to Colton to tap the resources of the police and locate the limousine in which Sampson disappeared. Colton ultimately provide an important lead. But he provides more than information. Colton reminds Archer of the authorities legitimate claims in the Sampson affair. Colton warns Archer about how dangerous Dwight Troy is, reminding the detective that there are limits to his strength and ability.

---

[48]Macdonald, <u>The Moving Target</u>, p. 139.

44

Humphreys, the local district attorney "with the lean face and haunted eyes of an intellectual sharp shooter,"[49] serves a similar function. He contrasts with Sheriff Spanner by his social class, intelligence, competence, and respect for Archer's abilities. Humphreys intervenes when Archer argues that Sampson may be killed by the kidnappers if the sheriff arrests whoever picks up the ransom. "It's not good law enforcement but we've got to conpromise. The thing is to save Sampson's life."[50]

Humphreys reminds the sheriff that slavish obedience to the rules won't solve the problem they face. Their solutions must be worked out with an awareness to the forces of external reality which include the possible actions of the kidnappers.

An Apprentice Ego

Throughout the novel, Archer functions as the ego center of the tale. As we have seen, he models the possibility of rationally balancing the forces of id, superego, and external reality. And he does this for more than the reader alone.

In Miranda Sampson, Macdonald combines two figures who occur regularly in his fiction: the young person in need of both rescue from some immediate danger and passage into adult autonomy, and the sexually appealing and vulnerable woman. The purpose of her sexual presence is not so much as a sexual object for the hero but, having made clear that she represents a real temptation, to display his renunciatory power.[51]

---

[49]Ibid., p. 100.

[50]Ibid., p. 101.

[51]Jewett and Lawrence suggest that this "separation of sexual relationships from the most important personal values of a hero" is a recuring process in popular culture which makes "permanent sexual commitments impossible." (American Monomyth, New York: Double Day, 1977, p. 251).

Archer's renunciation of a sexual relationship with Miranda enables the detective to serve her as the instructor of youth. He speaks to her of the responsibilities of her sexuality.[52] He tells her of the need to allow herself time to grow up, "You can't speed up time. You have to pick up its beat and let it support you."[53] And he urges her toward autonomy, "You're on your own . . . you've got to get out of this house and look after yourself."[54] Her father's wealth has enabled Miranda to pursue her desires, but it has kept her from accepting adult independence and responsibility. Archer's role is that of counselor and adviser guiding her in the direction of independence.

As with so many of the young people in subsequent Archer novels, Miranda Sampson serves as an apprentice ego. Archer ushers her out of an id dominated state into healthy adult ego balance through their search for her troubled and troubling, and quite repressed, superego (Sampson). This seems to be Archer's only real success since he fails to prevent Ralph Sampson's murder.[55]

At twenty or twenty-one Miranda seems unfinished with adolescence. Archer describes her as " a tall girl, whose movements had a certain awkward charm"[56] Uncertain, a Radcliffe dropout, she lacks the life experience that will make her an adult. This can be seen in her uncertainty about how to deal with her sexuality. She is infatuated with the handsome young war hero, Alan Taggert, and sought by Albert Graves; "It was triangle, but not an equilateral

---

[52]Macdonald, The Moving Target, p. 75.

[53]Ibid., p. 83.

[54]Ibid., p. 180.

[55]Note that the actual client of rcord, Elaine Sampson, gets what she says she wants - her husband's death and her own subsequent inheritance.

[56]Macdonald, The Moving Target, p. 8.

one."[57] Miranda's inexperience is confirmed when Taggert and Archer each refuse to take seriously her analysis of Elaine and Ralph Sampson. Both the pilot and later the detective suggest that she has been "reading books,"[58] as though her understanding was rooted in the ideas of others rather than in her experience of life with her father and step-mother.

Already uncertain, living a prolonged adolescence in a difficult home situation with a disintegrating father and spiteful step-mother, she suffers three great blows during the tale: Taggert's death, her father's murder, and her discovery of Albert Graves' guilt. It is Archer who ushers her through this difficult time, who at each stage brings her news, who offers her comfort and advice. This passage into adulthood requires that Miranda deal with these blows and with her own sexuality when Archer tells her of Taggert's death. She turns the conversation to the pass she made at Archer earlier, as though the pass and Taggert's death were connected, and then flees to Albert Graves - seeking out, in her confusion, the sexual love of a father figure.[59] By the end of the tale, the quick succession of her father's death, her discovery of Grave's guilt, and his confession and arrest prevent the consumation of Miranda's marriage to the attorney.[60]

Both Miranda and Archer seem to see their relationship as instructive or therapeutic. She comes to treat the detective almost as a confessor, most obviously when, following her fight with Elaine and again during their trip to the Temple in the Clouds, she talks to Archer about her family life and sexuality.

When all is said and done, the detective's advice to Miranda is to follow the route of autonomy, "You're

---

[57]Ibid., p. 16.

[58]Ibid., pp. 8 & 88.

[59]Ibid., see pp. 144-45.

[60]Ibid., see Chapter 31.

on your own . . . you've got to get out of this house and look after yourself."[61] He urges her, in effect, to follow his example and take rational ego control of her life and balance the forces which come to bear upon it.

The detective's sexual reticence toward Miranda underscores his understanding of their relationship. Though his attraction to the young woman is evident, he restrains his impulses, at least in part in recognition of the special ethical demands inherent in the role he has taken on. At the end of the novel, when she is at her most vulnerable and comes to Archer for comfort, he recognizes

I could have put my arms around her and taken her over. She was that lost, that vulnerable. But if I had, she'd have hated me in a week. In six months I might have hated Miranda.[62]

Archer sees Miranda through a difficult time, models for her the possibility of taking ego control, advises her, and turns her loose at the end of the novel. Asked in The Way Some People Die, to pass on someone's love to Miranda, Archer says "I never see her. She moved to Hawaii."[63] One assumes that there she has matured and achieved ego control of her life.

4) Conclusions

While others of his generation, such as John D. MacDonald and Mickey Spillane, have enjoyed broader popular followings, it was Ross Macdonald who was accepted as one of their own by "serious" writers, literary critics, and traditional academics.[64] A

---

[61]Ibid., p. 180.

[62]Ibid., p. 184.

[63]John Ross Macdonald, The Way Some People Die (New York: Pocket Books, 1952), p. 63.

[64]See the discussion of Macdonald's literary reputation in my bibliographic essay, "Explorations of Lew Archer," Clues 8:2, Winter '87.

Freudian approach to his work suggests some reasons why it is Macdonald rather than these more popular practicioners of the genre who is recognized as the intellectual's hard-boiled writer.

Macdonald's literary reputation has usually been credited to his erudition, style, and command of simile. Certainly these literary attributes are important, but a Freudian approach helps us to see the context of social psychology in which Macdonald's work came to be appreciated. Macdonald's novels combine a style pleasing to an erudite audience with a content shaped by displaced wish fulfillment and the exploration and resolution of psychic and social tensions. With this combination, Macdonald offers literary satisfactions which appeal particularly to the intellectual class.

The hard-boiled detective story is a hybrid, combining elements of the mystery and adventure formulas. The hard-boiled hero uses both action and intellect to resolve his cases, and different authors make different choices about the balance between the two qualities. Even at the beginning of the Archer series it is evident that Macdonald will draw on action while allowing the intellect to dominate. Lew Archer's adventures require that he face danger, and though not a violent man, he has the physical competence necessary to his calling. But clearly analysis and evaluation are more useful skills to Archer than any ability with fists or guns.

For the reader who identifies with Archer, there is a double pleasure to be had in the detective's apparent superiority to the the possessors of the more traditional fruits of erotic and ambitious fantasy. First the tale allows the reader the pleasure of imagining through secondary characters the release of the id's erotic and ambitious wishes. But the persons who have what the fantasizer lacks suffer for what they have obtained. And this leads to the second pleasure, the "sour grapes" satisfaction which allows the reader the pleasure of considering and rejectiong the satisfactions he or she is unable to obtain. One may then deny one's interest in the wealth and authority that one is dined. The fantasizer imagines that, like the hero, he or she has considered and rejected these satisfactions.

It should not suprise us to find that these tales are popular with the intellectual class, that is academics, artists, critics, and the consumers of their work. Archer is the ego center of his tale and his ability to bring the rational restraints of the ego to bear upon the forces of the id and superego makes him a fantasy figure aligned with the interests of an audience committed to authority of the rational. Archer has the physical ability to respond in kind to the irrational forces of the superego but chooses to use the power of ironic wit instead. An action fiction that grants the rational mind ultimate authority over brute force has great appeal to intellectuals who live in a culture which affirms the life of action. A fantasy in which the fantasizer can imagine renouncing the power which s/he does not in fact have is deeply satisfying.

The intellectual class has a unique place in society. They accept the renunciation of the more direct satisfaction of erotic and ambitious desires in the pursuit of the aesthetic path to happiness.[65] Freud suggests that "this aesthetic attitude to the goal of life offers little protection against the threat of suffering, but it can compensate for a great deal."[66] The intellectual, who sees the upper classes freely pursuing ambitious satisfactions and at least imagines that the lower classes enjoy erotic satisfaction unencumbered by social and ethical restraint, receives as the reward for his or her renunciations aesthetic satisfactions which are not clearly understood or appreciated by others in society. Archer is presented as one who has gone among all classes, considered the conventional satisfactions available to each, and chosen the "better way" of the intellectual's renunciations. But the structure of the fantasy is such that he continues to be respected by those whose choices are different from his own,

---

[65]Which Freud regards as "a displacement of the sexual." Freud, <u>Civilization and its Discontents</u>, p. 28.

[66]<u>Ibid</u>., p. 29.

and he is thus affirmed as a wise man who is able to lead others to an enlightened life in the world.

A fantasy in which an action hero, who can be seen as a displacement of the reader, acts with power and authority while using the gifts of the intellectual, has obvious appeal to the intellectual class.

In total, Macdonald's style, the displacement of the pleasures of wish fulfillment, the character of the protagonist, and conflicts with which he is confronted, combine to create fiction which confirms the intellectual's values and the renunciations s/he has accepted. This allows the identification with a hero who resolves adventure situations by the processes of the intellect.

Hard-boiled detective novels - especially those of Ross Macdonald - do lend themselves to Freudian analysis. Considered in this way, we see more clearly the tales social function. A part of their appeal lies in the presentation, through the protagonist's struggles, of the victory of the ego over forces which we recognize from our own unconscious life. A further appeal is to be found in the way that erotic and ambitious wishes are given expression and judged. Finally, in Macdonald's case, the intellectual processes by which the detective solves crimes and the reasoning required in setting aside erotic and ambitious desires would seem to restrict the appeal of Macdonald's work to a narrower audience than that found by the films based on his books or on the work of writers less interested in renunciation.

CHAPTER THREE
THE ETHICS OF RESPONSIBILITY IN THE UNDERGROUND MAN

Theologian and ethicist H. Richard Niebuhr[1] argues that the concept of responsibility has shaped contemporary ethical thought in both academic and popular ciricles. Niebuhr developed the idea of responsibility in The Responsible Self[2] as a source for ethics double purpose: self knowledge and guidance for our action.

Using this concept of responsibility The Underground Man can be viewed as a moral fiction with Lew Archer at its core. Ross Macdonald presents Archer as essentially cut off from others, yet the resolution of relationship is at the heart of the detective's method. The conclusion of his tales presents to others the possibility of new or renewed relationships based on mutual responsibility.

Niebuhr suggests that responsibility has had its modern meaning, whereby we may speak of the detective's responsibility to his client and to the higher law, only in the Nineteenth and Twentieth

---

[1]With his brother Reinhold, H. Richard Niebuhr (1894-1962) was one of the major figures in Twentieth Century Protestant thought. A pastor and teacher, Niebuhr joined the faculty of Yale in 1931, authored nine books and 60 articles, and trained several generations of pastors and teachers.

[2]Originally presented as the Robertson Lecture at Glasgow University in 1960 these lectures, with some supplemental materials, make up what James Gustafson called the only "development of his [Niebuhr's] systematic ethics that had been written in publishable form by the time of his death." (See Gustafson's "Forward" to Libertus A. Hoedemaker, The Theology of H. Richard Niebuhr (New York: Pilgrim Press, 1970), p. v.

Centuries. In modern times the concept is used in ethical reflection which in the past would have been guided by terms such as the good or the moral.[3] To define the concept more clearly than it has been in common usage, and to clarify its difference from more traditional ethical symbols. Niebuhr contrasts the image of the person as (responsible) answerer to the classical symbols of maker and citizen.

The image of the maker informs purposive (ontological) ethics. Such an approach focuses on means and ends and asks, "What is the goal to be achieved?" The image of the citizen undergirds deontological ethics and focuses on mores and rules and asks, "What is the rule to be obeyed?" The symbol of the responsible answerer is neither simply a new way of raising these traditional questions nor a synthesis of the approaches. Confronted with the question, what shall I do, responsibility asks at the point of every decision "What is going on?"[4]

Niebuhr's image of the answerer lends itself more readily to the discussion of the detective story than do more traditional ethical formulas. Niebuhr suggests that, with the symbol of the answerer, we consider "our actions as having the pattern of what we do when we answer another who addresses us."[5] Life is like an ongoing dialogue in which our response is predicated on our interpretation of the actions and potential reactions of the other, and on our sense of obligation to a valuing community of others against which we judge our actions. In the moral life then the action "that fits into a total interaction as response and as anticipation of further response, is alone conducive to the good and alone is right."[6]

---

[3]See The Responsible Self, (New York: Harper and Row, 1963) p. 47.

[4]Ibid., p. 60.

[5]Ibid.

[6]Ibid., p. 61.

The traditional ethical symbol of the citizen might be used in considering crime fiction since that symbol focuses on the question of law. But, the consideration of Chandler's The Long Goodbye in Chapter One demonstrates the limits of such an approach. The violation for which Marlowe pursues Terry Lennox is the abuse of friendship, not his crimes of murder and robbery. Crime is not the root problem in the mystery story, but the expression of that problem and the mechanism by which the underlying issues are exposed. Alternately, one might say that Marlowe is motivated by the ontological goal or ideal of a manly friendship but such a reading obscures the twisting nature of the mystery plot and the way in which the situation seems to force itself upon the protagonist without the element of choosing implied in the image of the maker.

The greatest advantage of the application of the question of responsibility may be its avoidance of the implication of stasis in the moral life. The symbol of the answerer confronts the constantly changing character of the ethical situation and the need to constantly seek - not a single fitting response - but a series of fitting responses. Both rule and goal are but a part of the data considered in answering first, "What is going on?," and secondly, "What shall I do?"

Hammett's The Maltese Falcon provides a well known example in which detective Sam Spade must respond fittingly to the constantly changing character of the ethical situation: the death of his partner, a dishonest client, and several competing alternative clients, none of whom clearly identify the goal which drives them. In this constantly changing situation, Spade's evaluations must remain relative and subject to correction as he continues to inquire into "what is going on?" As we shall see, Archer is involved in a similarly complex dialogue in The Underground Man. The ethical dialogue is never finished, for each new encounter renews the conversation. Hoedemaker writes, ". . . There is no solution except the solution which is expressed and re-expressed in particular decisions."[7]

---

[7]Hoedemaker, p. 91.

Marlowe, Archer, and their fellows pursue the question "What is going on?" while searching for the fitting reply. And if this symbol is indeed central to ethical reflection in the modern world then the root mystery which draws us to the tale may indeed be the mystery of Being itself.

In this chapter, 1) Niebuhr's ethical model of responsible dialogue is examined as a way to understand the ethical structures of the hard-boiled detective, 2) The Underground Man is examined in relationship to this model, and 3) it is concluded that responsibility is the underlying ethical model in The Underground Man and that a dialectical tension between the detective's values and culture limits the tale's ability to critique society or call for substantive changes.

1) Responsible Dialogue

All action may be thought of as response to action upon us. What makes response an ethical model is the ideal of responsible dialogue. Niebuhr suggests four tests of responsibility. The criteria of responsibility are met when: 1) our action responds to "interpreted action upon us,"[8] 2) that response is "in accordance with our interpretation of the question to which our answer is being given,"[9] 3) the action anticipates the "answers to our answers,"[10] and 4) all this happens in an ongoing "discourse . . . among beings forming a continuing society."[11]

Consider Archer's account of a single moment in the first chapter of The Underground Man. Stanley Broadhurst finds his five- or six-year-old son, Ronny, feeding the blue jays with Archer and says to the detective:

---

[8]Niebuhr, p. 61.

[9]Ibid., p. 63.

[10]Ibid., p. 64.

[11]Ibid., p. 65.

56

'. . . keep your dirty hands off him.'

> I was tempted to slug the man, But it wouldn't do the boy any good, and it wouldn't do the woman any good.[12]

Stanley's remark is an action upon Archer to which the detective must respond. But Archer interprets the remark as Stanley's inappropriate response to the situation he finds. Archer forsees Stanley's response to the action Archer contemplates and, accepting a social tie to the boy and his mother, does not "slug the man." This simple incident itself takes place in a larger dialogue where Stanley's action is a response to having been left by Jean Broadhurst. In turn it is a part of a dialogue between Archer and the boy which will require Archer's subsequent response to the boy's disappearance.

We have our being within a particular community. Even one who stands apart from society, as Archer often does, stands apart from a particular society and is thus shaped by it. We experience community both as a given and, perhaps to a lesser extent, as a chosen source of obligation. The opening chapter of The Underground Man, with its interactions between Archer, Ronny, and the boy's parents, establishes a tie to the Broadhursts which requires Archer's subsequent involvement.

In any situation, value is experienced both in relationship to the immediate community involved and to other, broader communities to which the self experiences the claim of loyalty. This is particularly evident within mystery fiction in the conflict between loyalty to a friend and to a larger community of moral obligation. This conflict of loyalties can be seen especially clearly in the final scene of the film of Harper in which the detective struggles with his loyalty and affection for Albert Graves and his recognition of Graves' crime.

A center of value is needed by which the conflicting claims of loyalty can be mediated.

---

[12]Ross Macdonald, The Underground Man (New York: Bantam, 1972), p. 4.

Niebuhr calls this center of value the individual's religion, that is, his or her cause, the source of ultimate commitment. Most people live as polytheists with multiple sources of demand, others limit their loyalty to some narrowly focused community such as their national, ethnic, or religous community. That is, from the many they elevate a single limited source of demand. Niebuhr says that this personal and societal divided loyalty is contrasted by an urge to unity, a seed of integrity expressed in a sense of universal responsibility. But what in that pantheon of demands upon us makes real that internal unity. Where is "one among all the many."[13]

Niebuhr sees one beyond the many who is the source of being itself and whom Christians experience as God revealed through Jesus Christ. But no specific religion solely expresses the community of being itself in which ultimate claim is experienced and through which all other claims are judged. This experience of accountability happens both in relationship to a particular community and independent from one's immediate companions because the individual recognizes that he or she simultaneously belongs to another, wider pattern. Ultimately for Niebuhr the individual is accountable to the community of being itself.

What binds the individual to a particular community, beyond the happenstance of history, is the acceptance of some common cause or object of devotion. For the patriot it may be trust in some system of government as a source of value. For the academic, and perhaps for the fictional detective as well, it may be the pursuit of truth which binds the self into a community of faith with others who share in loyalty to that end. The cause is both personal and impersonal. It is embodied in others of the present community, modeled by those who preceeded us in faithfulness to our cause (i.e., the saints). It exists also as disembodied ideal. We may speak of conscience as the voice of this community judging our faithfulness to its cause.[14]

---

[13]Niebuhr, p. 139.

[14]See Niebuhr, pp. 78 - 79.

This image of responsibility to a community oversimplifies the ethical dilemma if we do not recognize that modern people live within many communities and that the various demands of these communities are not in harmony with each other. The detective's tale exposes the multitude of demands which the individual faces. For instance, in Hammett's The Maltese Falcon, Brigid O'Shaughnessy's demand that Spade provide her with the protection due a client and lover is at odds with the demand Spade feels to be true to his now dead partner and, in a different way, with the demand of the law upon a citizen. Niebuhr spoke to this problem of the multiple systems of demand which we experience when he wrote, "I protest against this inner manifoldness by turning from the many systems of action upon myself."[15]

Niebuhr's answer to this protest is found in montheistic faith. Without some larger claim against which to measure the demand of the community, there is a great temptation to collapse the dialectic between self and community and lapse into social faith, to surrender the search for the fitting response to the authority of the group. When we escape into the mass in this way we replace the I of selfhood with the impersonal direction one, as in the charge "It is fitting that one should . . ." The community comes to stand between the self and being itself and the individual becomes one of the many.

Timeful Responsibility

The answerer has being in relation to time and history as well as to contemporary society. In being known the self "is timeful in ways of which teleology and ontology seem unaware."[16] We are historically relative beings. In The Theology of H. Richard Niebuhr Hoedemaker speaks of this by noting that "'man is in time' . . . the present of the self contains a past and a future, not a past and a future of facts but of deeds and sufferings, hopes and expecta-

---

[15]Ibid., p. 138.

[16]Ibid., p. 93.

tions.[17] But as much as we are in time, Hoedemaker continues, time is in us. "Time-in-man points to the riddle of his inexplicable thereness, his finitude, conditionedness, restrictedness, and dependence."[18]

As was noted above, society is itself experienced timefully. When I am faithful to a community I am bound not only to those who presently make up the community but to those who preceeded me in the community and whose words and actions are recalled as examples of the community at its best. Thus the American patriot continues to be in dialogue with Jefferson, Lincoln, and King as well as with contemporary persons.

The responsible self's responses in the present are shaped both by a shared and a personal past and by hope and expectation for the future. Archer's divorce and its painful judgement on his life and career (which the film _Harper_ moves into the tales present) is an example of the timefullness of our response to the present. This timeful self does not respond with interpretations based on pure reason or an absolute philosophical ideal.

It comes rather with images and patterns of interpretation, with attitudes of trust and suspicion, accumulated in its biographical and historical past.[19]

But, while profoundly influenced by the past, a responsible act in the present is not bound by the past. Niebuhr holds out the possibility that we are not doomed simply to repeat the old animosities. Hope for the future rests in part on our ability to reconstruct the past. Rather as analytic psychology reinterprets the personal past, so the alienations of the social past must also be judged and reorganized.

Mickey Spillane's detective hero Mike Hammer is responsible after a fashion, but the history he

---

[17]Hodemaker, p. 69.

[18]_Ibid_., p. 70.

[19]Niebuhr, pp. 95-96.

claims as his own seems to begin with World War II and end with the Cold War. And the community to which he gives himself begins with the former war buddies and his secretary Velda who are his immediate companions and ends with an anti-communist and misogynist understanding of the nation state. Archer is a more complicated character because he is responsible within a larger, more inclusive community. "The responsible self is driven . . . to respond and be accountable in nothing less than a universal community."[20] Archer is not so idealized a hero that he conforms without conflict to the community of being itself. Archer is himself presented as a social and historical being shaped by his past; but, as he moves through the lives of his clients, he represents as detective the possiblity of reevaluating the past in light of a community broader than that of the client's immediate fellows. Before we finish we will want to consider the nature of the continuing society to which Archer is himself answerable.

A relationship was established with Ronny Broadhurst when they fed the blue jays together in The Underground Man. It is responsibility to this relationship which leads Archer to agree to be hired to return the boy to his mother. The search for Ronny leads the detective through a series of relationships which are distorted by the secrets of the past. As we shall see, it is not so much the evil done in the past as the keeping of secrets, the failure to confront the evil which was done, which binds the actors in the present.

At the end of The Underground Man, Archer reflects on Stanley's inability to resolve the past in ways which enable his action in the present.

I hoped that Ronny's life wouldn't turn back toward his father's death as his father's life had turned, in a narrowing circle. I wished the boy a benign failure of memory.[21]

_____

[20]Ibid., p. 88.

[21]Macdonald, The Underground Man, p. 249.

But such a failure of memory is unlikely. What is needed is the reinterpretation of the past, of the relationship to the father, in a wider context of being in which the father's limits and actions may be judged less personally so that the son may aspire to a different set of relationships. Those who have stressed the psychological structure of Macdonald's work have pointed to the necessary restructuring of the personal past. What is less clearly explored by Macdonald is the possibility that as a community it may be possible to reinterpret and revalue the social past.

Monotheistic Faith and Resposibility

The idea that historical and social relativity are central to the human condition runs throughout Niebuhr's work.[22] This relativity defines the context within which we make moral choices, for there is no place outside of our social/historical position from which we may critique our moral lives. Further, because of the multiplicity of communities within which we find ourselves, we experience multiple sources of demand which may be at odds with each other. How then is it possible to have an ethical standard whose cause is greater than narrowly defined self interest? And how shall we choose from the many demands upon our loyalty?

In making a moral choice we at least tacitly acknowledge some ultimate community to which we give our loyalty. For Neibuhr that which has ultimate claim on our lives is our religion. He suggests that our "religion" can be divided into three categories.[23] The polytheist acknowledges varied authorities in different contexts and thus declines to choose among them. Niebuhr calls his second category henotheism. The henotheist chooses one demand among the many and serves it. In The Underground Man, Captain Broadhurst's commitment to hedonism and Mrs. Snow's distorted commitment to protecting her son are both examples of the choice of the one among

---

[22]See especially, H. Richard Niebuhr, The Meaning of Revelation (New York: Macmillan, 1941).

[23]See Hoedemaker, p. 10.

the many. But it is only monotheism with its search for the one demand beyond the many, which provides a community and history broad enough to inform decision making which is responsible to being itself. Only such a cause judges each of the many demands upon us.

The monotheist does not judge his or her actions, and those of others, against the demand of any limited community but against the posited community of being itself in which everything that is has value. Niebuhr argues that the montheistic believer must see his or her responses to others as interrelated with responses to the center of the universal community - that is to God as the ultimate person and cause. Viewed in this way the responsive life is "a movement of self-judgement and self-guidance which cannot come to rest until it makes its reference to a universal community."[24]

It is here that Niebuhr's ethic of responsibility raises the greatest questions about Macdonald's fiction. For Niebuhr suggests that responsibility is known in loyalty to some community, and that monotheistic responsibility rests on loyalty to the community of being itself. The concept of responsibility does seem to shape the ethical discourse of the Archer novels. And the ethical standard which underlies the responsible dialogue of the tales is not simply that of the society in which they take place. But it is not clear what community supports and upholds Archer in his decisions.

One might argue that Archer is a literary hero and his ability to withstand ethical temptation simply expresses the author's romanticism. Certainly there is nothing wrong with a romantic fiction, though it is difficult to apply its discussions of the moral life to our own lives.

Recognized as a fictional character, Archer may be placed within a larger community which holds him to an ethical standard of responsibility. That community is obvious, however, only when we remember that Archer is a literary protagonist. As such he takes his place among a community of the faithful within the literary tradition within which he exists.

---

[24]Niebuhr, The Responsible Self, pp. 87

Dashiell Hammett's Continental Op, Raymond Chandler's Philip Marlowe, and even Mickey Spillane's Mike Hammer constitute the community to whom Archer must be faithful. His community is that of the genre which provides the historical context within which the character understands the demands upon him. Macdonald after all, names his detective after the partner of Hammett's Sam Spade. It is not far from Spade's insistence after Miles Archer's death that "When a man's partner is killed he's supposed to do something about it,"[25] to Lew Archer's readiness to seek out the boy to whom he said, "It's all right with me,"[26] when the child wanted to come outside and feed the blue jays.

Such a community may be said to exist. But it is ultimately an aesthetic community which exisits only as a set of conventions recognized by the readers and writers of detective fiction rather than one which is recognized anywhere (except in comedy) by its supposed participants.

Archer, like other hard-boiled detectives, is a loner with a highly developed sense of loyalty.[27] The question which the Niebuhrian must ask is, to what is Archer loyal, and specifically, is that loyalty to being itself?

There are hints at a monotheistic loyalty in Macdonald's work. The detective's conventional refusal to limit his loyalty to what is contractually demanded, and the struggle to define his obligation to the police - and through them to the particular society in which the detective lives - suggests that he is

---

[25]Dashiell Hammett, The Maltese Falcon (New York: Vintage Books, 1972) p. 193.

[26]Macdonald, The Underground Man, p. 1.

[27]It may be the detective's sense of responsibility which keeps him a loner. Others are unable to live up to the detective's standards and he does not seem to find it worth the price of maintaining relationships. Yet something keeps him from giving up utterly on others and draws him into responsible, if short-term, relationships with clients.

not primarily motivated by societal obligation. Macdonald's environmentalism and the criticism of racial prejudice implicit, and occasionally explicit, in his work point to some wider loyalty.

In The Underground Man, the source of Archer's sense of obligation is Ronny Broadhurst rather than the fee he may earn or even the potential romantic/sexual relationship with the boy's mother.[28] Archer limits his obligation to those who have penetrated his distance and established relationship with him. To such persons Archer accepts no limit to his loyalty. But, while he may disapprove of racism, the destruction of the environment, and even of the crimes and distortions of justice he observes, Archer is most likely to remain silent or offer a minimal protest. The detective's loyalty to being itself is limited by his loyalty to the purity of his own image. Thus the tales, which hint at some form of individualism, lack monotheism's commitment to the goodness of everything that is. In Macdonald's moral universe relationship limits responsibility.

Sin and Suffering

In Niebuhr's ethics of responsibility, sin is understood as all that falls short of radical monotheism, that is all that denies the oneness and goodness of God. This disloyalty to the one beyond the many has both religous and social or communal dimensions. The disloyalty of individuals to the One on whom we are dependent, which is manifest in the choice of the lesser good, may be spoken of as a religious matter. But Niebuhr never entirely abandons the social gospel movement's awareness of the way sin becomes incarnate in group structures.

In Macdonald's novels, and perhaps in the detective story in general, the detective's investigations reveal the choices made in the past which have resulted

---

[28]Typical of the tendency in film to make romance the source of motivation and obligation, in the film based on the novel, (Underground Man) the source of Archer's moral obligation is transferred from Ronny Broadhurst himself to a past romance with his mother.

in the problems of the present.[29] This process tends
to focus on individual sins. But behind these personal
sins lies the social expression of sin and it too
is often uncovered. In Macdonald's work there are
three obvious areas in which this social sin is
revealed. The burden which young people, such as
Jerry Kilpatrick in The Underground Man, carry is
often an expression of what is wrong with society
as a whole. In the recurring environmental concern
especially evident in The Sleeping Beauty and in
The Drowning Pool Macdonald uses the oil industry
as an example of the way that greed, that is
glorified self-interest, takes over institutions.
Finally, the police, themselves charged with
maintaining the law, often represent institu-
tionalized sin when they place self-interest or some
narrow loyalty above the common good.

Sin is a universal and inevitable phenomenon
of human life. None of us is wholy true to being
itself. Radical monotheism with its commitment to
the universal community of being reveals both an
ethical ideal and a rule by which to test faithfulness
to that ideal. Because sin is universal, suffering
is inevitable. If God is the one beyond the many,
the divine presence must be active in all our
experience. This does not require that we believe
that God causes our suffering in order to teach us
some lesson. But radical monotheism cannot exempt
God from involvment, and indeed responsibility, in
the situation. Ottati argues that,

> Though he nowhere explicitly states it, one
> implication of Niebuhr's analysis of social
> tragedy and personal suffering is that a
> teleological scheme has difficulty accounting
> for God's ordering and judging in apparent evil.[30]

---

[29]For example, in The Underground Man, the
actions in the present of Stanley Broadhurst,
Al Sweetner, Mrs. Snow, and Brian Kilpatrick are
determined in large part by the decisions they made
at the time of Leo Broadhurst's death.

[30]Douglas F. Ottati, Meaning and Method
in H. Richard Niebuhr's Theology (Washington
D.C.:University Press of America, 1982), p. 151.

Teleology, with its emphasis on the human agent as maker, cannot adequately deal with the biblical conviction that God acts upon us in all that we experience which is given expression in the call to read the signs of the times and respond accordingly. For the radical monotheist every situation, including suffering, is a part of the ongoing dialogue with the One beyond the many. Though it would be obscene to reflect on an experience such as the Holocaust as though suffering were justified by the growth of character which may result, still the responsible self must reflect on the totality of experience. Thus Niebuhr does not write that people's character is formed simply by what has happened to them but even more importantly by their own responses to what happened to them, "and these responses have been shaped by their interpretation of what they suffered."[31]

Consider the end of The Underground Man and Archer's hope "that Ronny's life wouldn't turn back toward his father's death as his father's life had turned in a narrowing circle."[32] The sufferings of both Ronny and his father, Stanley, were inflicted by the choices their fathers made. That situation is a fact of their existence. Stanley was unable to expand his dialogue of response to a context wider than his relationship with his father and this narowing circle crippled his other relationships and led to the dissolution of his marriage and ultimately to his death. This literal death within the tale points to a figurative death which is the price of the inability to embrace the widest possible community of response and value. For Ronny Broadhurst to overcome, and even make use of his suffering, he must consider it yet another sort of action impinging upon him which warrants interpretation and fitting response.

Restraining Others

---

[31]Niebuhr, Responsible Self, p. 59.

[32]Macdonald, The Underground Man, p. 249.

The moral life is not experienced in isolation from others, and the questions of right relationship are questions which societies as well as individuals must resolve. In the community of being itself all have equal value before the One beyond the many. But they will have relative values for the individual. Niebuhr observes that "Priest, Levite, and Samaritan must be considered equal in value as objects of divine valuation; but they are not equal in value to the victim of the robbers."[33]

The search for relative justice in society requires the balancing of the individual's relative and ultimate value. When this is accomplished it makes possible "the formulation and reformation of relative judgements by reference to the absolute relationship."[34] Archer's interaction with others suggests that it is to this dual valuation that he refers when he says "most of my work is watching people, and judging them."[35]

The search for justice is a part of the struggle for a right (i.e., responsible) relationship between various groups, or parts, of society. And it is not just wronged individuals who are served by this search. In Radical Monotheism, Niebuhr says "a just-right relationship between such parts must be sought in order that the society may live and realize its potentialities."[36]

Both the social character of sin, and the fact that individual sin is acted out against others raise the question of whether our responses may at times involve the restraint of the other. I take the restraining of others to be an issue which determines

---

[33]H. Richard Niebuhr, Christ and Culture (New York: Harper Colophon, 1975), p. 237.

[34]Ibid., p. 240.

[35]Ross Macdonald, The Moving Target, (New York: Bantam, 1970), p. 82.

[36]H. Richard Niebuhr, Radical Monotheism and Western Culture: With Supplemental Essays (New York: Harper Torchbooks, 1970), p. 102.

whether "responsibility" can become a fitting symbol for a social as well as a personal ethic. The responsible agent acts within a community of interaction. The agent is responsible, not simply for his or her own actions, but for the interactions within which responsibility is known. In such a system the possibility of restraining, at some point, the actions of another presents itself. Consistent monotheism points to the possibility of both restraining and being restrained. We are more likely to see the detective hero restraining than being restrained. But if the hero's actions enforce an obligation by which he and his client as well as the other are bound, then the possibility of being restrained is at least implied.[37] The possibility of restraining others raises the question of the use of force and of death as the ultimate restraint.

Within a tale any act of violence may be regarded as tragic and dehumanizing, or the tale may glorify certain uses of violence.[38] Whatever attitude is taken toward the larger question of violence, ethical distinctions will be made within the tale between different uses of violence.

The mystery story is not well served by the traditional ethical structures of rules and goals. Faced with the violent confrontations of the hard-boiled world neither the question of the end to be served nor of the applicable law may usefully guide the detective's actions. The symbol of responsibility brought to bear upon the violent interactions within the mystery tale raises the question of who is being restricted, for what purpose, and within what community

---

[37]Much of the hard-boiled detective's struggle with the police centers on defining the restraints to which the detective must submit.

[38]The attraction of literary violence lies in part in its clarity of resolution. In the detective story the symbol of violent confrontation is used to identify the moral problem at issue. There is a moral purity and simplicity in the destruction of a character who represents evil matched by no other solution, while the death of an innocent person functions as an ultimate transgression.

of meaning. Violence itself is an action which requires fitting reaction and the symbol of responsibility can help us to understand the distinctions made within the tale between different uses of force.

2) Narrative Analysis:
Responsible Relationship in the Underground Man

The ethical questions raised in The Responsible Self provide a rich textual reading of The Underground Man which reveals the moral assumptions therein. The answer to the mystery of The Underground Man should then be revealed through the uncovering of responsible relationship. This is to say more than simply that there is a moral conclusion to the tale in which the evil doer is revealed and punished. Rather, the tale is advanced by its exploration of the struggle with responsibility.

As in much of Macdonald's fiction, a family at the center of the tale is the testing ground for the possibility of responsible dialogical relationships. When Jean Broadhurst comes to Archer, she is seeking to reestablish a relationship which has been suddenly disrupted. But the detective's investigations reveal deeper disruptions which underly the dialogue of interaction. The immediate problem of what has become of young Ronny Broadhurst is only solved by solving the riddle of the disappearances of both his father, Stanley, and his grandfather, Captain Leo Broadhurst. The disappearances reveal, more than they cause, the broken dialogue which separates the various Broadhursts. But before Archer can attempt to solve these disappearances he must himself be drawn into a dialogue of interaction which will require him to be involved in the lives of the Broadhursts.

Narrative Units

The novel can be divided into narrative units based on spatial movement within the tale. Within these narrative units new relationships are introduced, new information about known and previously unknown relationships is revealed, and the quality of the relationships change. Through this evolutionary process, the truth about the past emerges and allows Archer to solve the mystery of the present.

1) The Opening Scene

In the opening scene, Archer's relationship with Ronny Broadhurst is established and his awareness of a potential romantic relationship with the boy's mother, Jean, is implied. The break in Jean's marriage to Stanley is revealed, though not yet explained. Stanley takes the boy, supposedly to visit Grandma Nell (Elizabeth Broadhurst), and leaves with a young blond (Sue Crandall) whose arrival had precipitated Jean's leaving Stanley the previous night. Already we have seen a family relationship threatened by the husband/father's unexplained obsessive behavior, and new relationships suggested between Archer and Ronny, Archer and Jean, and Stanley and the girl.

Any tale focusing on a professional detective will involve the establishment of the limited contractual relationship between detective and client.[39] But from the beginning Macdonald goes to great lengths to make clear that it is the relational demands rather than the fee which ties Archer to the Broadhursts. The novel's opening scene moves Archer from his singleness into relationship with the boy. This is not a case Archer wants and he first rejects the possibility of becoming involved, saying, "This is my day off. I hope."[40] But when Ronny asked him, "Is it all right if I come out?" Archer had replied, "It's all right with me."[41] That limited response begins a relationship so that Archer confesses that when Stanley takes his son and leaves, "I wanted to stop Broadhurst and bring the boy back. But I didn't."[42] Archer's responses to the case grow out of the obligation he experiences for what he has, and has not, done. Archer remains

---

[39]The conventional romanticism of the genre is often expressed by the detective's movement to a commitment to someone in the case which is greater than the contractual relationship. This often is expressed by the detective's refusal to be ordered off the case.

[40]Macdonald, The Underground Man, p. 5.

[41]Ibid., p. 1.

[42]Ibid., p. 6.

a professional and asks for a fee, but he chooses to enter into the case as the proper response to the relationship he has begun with the boy. Archer's act in accepting the case is an answer to action upon him by both Ronny and Stanley.

2) Archer is Hired
When Archer agrees to be hired by Jean Broadhurst, the reponsibility he already feels toward Ronny is formalized and transferred, in part, to Jean, who is now his client. As Archer goes with Jean to Elizabeth Broadhurst's, he learns of Stanley's father search. Stanley responds to his father's disappearance as an action toward him and his obsessive response has led to the break in his marriage. Here the case is clearly set within the context of a larger circle of relationship which will subsequently be examined.

3) At Jean and Stanley's House
Stopping at Jean and Stanley's home, Archer finds further evidence that Stanley's obsession has broken his marriage relationship, and objects (left there by Sue Crandall) which point to other broken relationship: a book with Ellen Strome's and Jerry Kilpatrick's names in it, and a Mercedes Benz registered to Roger Armistead. Here Al Sweetner enters the tale, demanding $1,000 which he says Stanley was to have gotten from his mother. Here the immediate break in relationship which Archer is examining is revealed to be a part of a larger pattern of broken relationships. Ronny takes his narrative place with Sue, Jerry, and Al in the circle of young people hurt by the impact of the secrets of the Mountain House on their childhood.

4) At the Broadhurst Ranch
At her ranch, Elizabeth Broadhurst asks Jean if Stanley has been having an affair (that is, an inappropriate relationship) with Sue Crandall. It is perhaps worth noting that it is his mother who raises the question of infidelity, which led to the disappearance of Stanley's father and which will shape relationships throughout the novel. At the ranch, Archer meets another wounded "child" in the gardener, retarded Fritz Snow. Fritz's retardation seems to reflect the retarded development of other characters who, like Fritz, cannot become adults because they cannot resolve their relationships with their parents.

5) At the Mountain House

Outside the cabin above the Broadhurst ranch, Archer finds Deputy Coroner Joe Kelsey investigating who is responsible for the forest fire. Kelsey questions Archer, and then shows him a newly buried body which Archer identifies as Stanley Broadhurst. Stanley has been killed with a pickaxe used to dig his grave and his cigarillo started the forest fire. Thus Stanley is immediately responsible for the real as well as the metaphorical fire which rages throughout the tale. But there are others who caused Stanley's actions. Later, Kelsey says, "Whoever killed him probably made him drop this (the cigarillo) in the dry grass. That means they're legally and financially responsible for the fire."[43] Together the two investigators rebury the body to protect it from the fire. Irresponsibility has claimed a life. Stanley is dead, and as we shall see, his murder and Ronny's disappearance can only be solved by seeing the web of responsible and irresponsible relationships which bind the characters.

6) Back at the Ranch

The Broadhurst women are told of Stanley's death and the disappearance of Ronny and Sue Crandall. This interlude serves to reunite Archer with Jean Broadhurst and to update the women and review for the reader the first death to be uncovered in the tale. Fleeing the fire Elizabeth, Jean, Kelsey and Archer go together to Mrs. Snow's house.

7) At Mrs. Snow's House

Here we meet the overly protective Mrs. Snow and Fritz admits to Archer that in return for a small sexual favor (again, an inappropriate, that is, less than honest and mutual, relationship) he let Sue take his car. The disintegrating relationships are too much for Elizabeth Broadhurst, who suffers a heart attack and is rushed to the hospital.

8) At the Armistead House

Archer returns the Mercedes to Mrs. Armistead and learns more about the link between Sue and the Armisteads. Jerry Kilpatrick, whose name was in the book Sue left at Stanley and Jean's house, crews on Mr. Armistead's yacht. At the Armistead's beach

---

[43]Macdonald, The Underground Man, p. 43.

house Mr. Armistead provides Sue's name and for the first time in the novel she is known as more than "the blond girl." He says that she came aboard with Jerry and, when questioned, Armistead denies having had an affair with her. But the strains of the Armistead's marriage are obvious. It is shown to be a marriage maintained by her money rather than by mutual respect and honesty.

The Armisteads, like Joe Kelsey, are largely peripheral to the plot. But in addition to their car and sailboat, their relationship provides a contemporary parallel to that of Leo and Elizabeth Broadhurst: an attractive but weak man marries a wealth woman who attempts to hold the marriage together by the force of her character. Archer and Fran Armistead discuss the couple's lack of children and childishness. Armistead taught Jerry Kilpatrick to sail and allowed Jerry to live aboard the boat but the relationship remains insubstantial. It is clear that whatever his intentions, Roger Armistead cannot be the surrogate father who might help Jerry in the passage into adulthood.

9) At the Marina
Archer finds Jerry Kilpatrick, Sue Crandall, and Ronny Broadhurst on the Armistead's boat. Before Archer can learn anything Jerry overpowers him and Jerry and Sue sail away with Ronny. Though wrong (that is, an inappropriate response to Archer's action toward him), Jerry clearly regard knocking Archer out as an expression of his protective relationship to Sue and Ronny and an appropriate response to the threats of the adult world. Archer's attempt at relationship fails to break the bond of distrust of the adult world which ties Jerry and Sue to each other and to Ronny, whom they believe they are protecting.

10) At the Kilpatrick House
Archer visits Jerry's father. Like Stanley Broadhurst, Jerry suffers from the break up of his parents' marriage, blames his father for the split, and suffers from his inability to have an appropriate relationship with his father. Brian Kilpatrick's defensiveness and inability to act express the brokenness of his relationship with his son and his own moral weakness. Archer's interview with Kilpatrick is interrupted by a burned-out homeowner who charges that Kilpatrick hid the fire danger when he developed the canyon subdivision. The

interruption reminds the reader of the fire and, though the homeowner speaks only of the fire damage, raises the question of the land developer's involvement in all that is before us.

11) Back to Jean and Stanley's House
Returning to Jean Broadhurst's home, Archer finds the murdered body of Al Sweetner in a wig and false beard. Like so much in the tale, Al is disguised, but the disguise itself proves to be a displacement of responsibility. Archer also finds an old newspaper ad Stanley placed picturing Captain Broadhurst and his unnamed lover and asking for information.

This narrative unit introduces a new murder and a new disappearance to be explained. It also introduces a new clue, the wig and false beard, which points to the web of hidden relationships which run throughout the tale.

12) At the Crandalls' House
Archer finds the worried parents of a lost, lonely girl (Sue) whom they do not know well. They are yet another family whose secrets from the past have ultimately separated them from their child.

13) At Al Sweetner's Motel Room
Al's traveling companion, a drug addict named Elegant, tells Archer that Sweetner fed Sue Crandall L.S.D. in search of some secret, that Al got money from Mrs. Snow, and that a woman in a large house outside of San Francisco was involved in the case in some way.

Sweetner has had a series of inappropriate and abusive relationships: his sexual/romantic involvement with someone whose addiction causes her to sell herself to buy drugs, the use of drugs and sexual abuse to get what he wants from Sue Crandall, and playing upon the obsessions of both Mrs. Snow and Stanley Broadhurst to extort money from them. In none of his relationships has Sweetner been a responsible agent, for his actions destroy every relationship. Al neither accepts the consequences of his actions which are expressed in the reactions of others nor looks forward in a present deed to the continued interaction. It is interesting to contrast Al to Leo Broadhurst. Captain Broadhurst's inappropriate relationships will be revealed to be the result of weakness, but Al is presented as a genuinely evil character.

Archer's interchange with Elegant is worth noting. He withholds the news of Al's death while he questions her. He is conscious that he uses her rather than being in relationship with Elegant, and when he gives her fifty dollars reports, "I was conscious of buying and being sold at the same time."[44] The interchange acknowledges the compromise with responsible selfhood which even a romantic hero like Archer makes in pursuit of a goal.

14) Back at the Kilpatrick House
    Brian Kilpatrick makes tentative steps toward disclousure and responsibility when, the next morning, he goes with Archer to report to the police that Jerry and Sue have taken Ronny and the boat. He reluctantly admits that the woman in Stanley's newspaper ad (see #11 above) is his ex-wife and that Jerry has seen the ad and contacted Stanley Broadhurst. The revelation of this secret of the past provides the information which will allow the solution to the mystery and the unraveling of the broken relationships of the present. A judgement on Kilpatrick's own moral character will be possible only when we see how fully he has admitted and resolved the relationships of the past (see #24 below).

15) At the Mountain House, A Third Time
    Archer joins Joe Kelsey and Jean Broadhurst. Archer and Kelsey exchange information. The deputy coroner reports that Stanley was stabbed before being hit with the pickaxe and Archer tells them of Al Sweetner's death. Kelsey suspects Fritz Snow, who during his late teens was convicted of statutory rape, is guilty of the murder. The exchange between Archer and Kelsey is particularly interesting because it reflects a suspension of the distrust which generically divides a private investigator from official law enforcement personnel.[45]

---

[44]Macdonald, The Underground Man, p. 105.

[45]The possibilty of a responsible relationship between the two, in spite of the separation inherent in their roles, marks an increasing complexity of relationship that was absent from The Moving Target/Harper, in which the detective makes jokes at the expense of the police officers. Both differ from The Drowning Pool, in which a more implicated

76

16) The Broadhurst Ranch, A Third Time

Archer takes Jean Broadhurst to her mother-in-law's house. There, among unpaid bills, he finds and reads a family history in which Elizabeth Broadhurst describesd her father as "a god."[46] Archer and Jean discuss the case and the way that the lack of resolution of Stanley's parents' marriage gradually squeezes out his own. In spite of the bills, Jean insists that Mrs. Broadhurst has plenty of money and mentions a real estate partnership with Brian Kilpatrick. The linking of Elizabeth Broadhurst and Brian Kilpatrick tightens the circle of relationships which bind The Underground Man together, while her compulsion about her own father broadens the pattern of obsessive child/parent relationships and roots Stanley's actions in his mother's identity as well as his father's.

Before leaving the Broadhurst ranch Archer arranges for a San Francisco detective to begin searching for the woman who gave Al Sweetner money.

17) Back at Mrs. Snow's

The search for the relationships of the past which bind the present continues at the Snow's. Reluctantly Mrs. Snow admits that it was she who gave Al Sweetner money (see #13 above) and even more reluctantly admits that Al had been a foster child in her home.

We now know that Mrs. Snow has a parental relationship with two of the novel's characters, Fritz and Al Sweetner. It becomes increasingly apparent that her protection of Fritz is principally self-serving. The foster child, Al, reflects her character without the surface morality which Mrs. Snow presents to the world. Both Al and his foster mother are corrupt, Al is actually the more honest of the two in his presentation of himself.

Before Leo Broadhurst's disappearance, while they were in high school, Al, Fritz, and a girl named

---

police officer and Archer resolve their relationship only at the end of the tale.

46Macdonald, The Underground Man, p. 132.

Marty Nickerson stole a car and went to Los Angeles. Underage Marty returned pregnant, Fritz was charged with the statutory rape referred to by Joe Kelsey (see #15 above) and served six months at a forestry camp. Al, who had been in trouble before, was imprisioned until he came of age, and Marty got off by marrying the man whose car they stole. Al returned the summer that Captain Broadhurst disappeared and stole a forestry service bulldozer from Fritz, causing Fritz to be fired and suffer a nervous breakdown.

While it seems that yet another circle of flawed relationships has been introduced we will see that their Los Angeles adventure is integral to the webb of relationships on which the mystery is suspended. This is still more information about the past which will lead Archer to resolve the present. Mrs. Snow explains that Ellen Strome Kilpatrick was Al, Fritz, and Marty's high school art teacher and that she carried on an affair with Captain Broadhurst at the mountain house and then the Broadhurst home. Mrs. Broadhurst must have known, and young Stanley asked about it. A postcard Marty once sent Fritz reveals that the man she married was Lester Crandall, and the baby, Sue.

18) In Sausalito
    As the relationships of the past begins to be clarified the present is reasserted by a phone call from Joe Kelsey. The Armistead's sloop is breaking up on a beach. Archer arrives and traces Sue, Jerry, and Ronny to a motel owned by Lester Crandall, where Archer learns that Ellen Kilpatrick is living in Sausalito as Ellen Storm, and then joins Ellen, who is expecting Jerry and the others. She tells him that when Captain Broadhurst disappeared, she had already gone to Nevada for a divorce and Leo failed to join her. She and Archer are joined by the Crandalls and moments later Jerry walks down the driveway. He sees them, calls out, and Sue drives away with Ronny. Archer pursues her and Ronny to the Golden Gate Bridge where she climbs over the cat walk railing. Archer picks up Ronny and talks Sue back onto the bridge. Sue has fled as far as she can and at the last moment of decision Archer draws her back from death and toward life and renewed relationship.

Sue tells Archer that outside the Mountain House Stanley was digging for a red sports car. She fled with Ronny when Stanley was murdered by a man with a black beard, long hair, and dark glasses. She also tells a confused tale of two other visits to the Mountain House, one as child when her mother killed someone and left her overnight in the loft, and once when Al Sweetner took her there in search of the memory and raped her. Ronny has been recovered and the tale climaxes on the bridge. But in Macdonald's fiction the specific mystery points to more universal mysteries. The secrets of the past, which must be resolved if the characters are to live responsibly in the present, have not been entirely answered and the tale continues as the pieces of the past are assembled.

19) Back at the Crandalls' House
Archer returns Sue to Lester and Martha Crandall, insisting that she needs psychiatric care. Privately, Martha Crandall admits that 15 years before (at the same time that Al Sweetner returned from the reformatory) she had quarreled with her husband and gone to Leo Broadhurst, who had been her lover and was Sue's father. As the evidence of Captain Broadhurst's infidelities multiplies, the secret of them draws those affected back to the Mountain House.

20) Ellen Storm's House in Sausalito
Archer tells Ellen Storm (nee Strome Kilpatrick) that Leo Broadhurst has probably been dead the whole fifteen years and about Marty Nickerson Crandall. He asks about the possibility that Mrs. Broadhurst might have killed her husband. Ellen tells him that, according to Jerry, his father blackmailed Mrs. Broadhurst in some way, forcing her to put up the land for the real estate development which is wiped out by the forest fire that rages throughout the novel.

21) The Mountain House, A Fourth Visit
After returning Ronny to his mother, Archer asks Kelsey to bring a bulldozer to the Mountain House. Under the hole Stanley had dug and been buried in, they find Leo Broadhurst buried in his red Porsche.

22) At Mrs. Snow's, A Fourth Visit
When confronted Fritz admits that he buried Leo and the car on that night fifteen years earlier and says Al Sweetner made him do it. Mrs. Snow tells Archer that on that fateful night Brian Kilpatrick told Mrs. Broadhurst that Leo had Marty hidden in the Mountain House, that Mrs. Broadhurst followed

Leo with a gun, that Stanley followed her, and mother and son returned together.

23) At the Hospital
Archer questions Mrs. Broadhurst in her hospital room. Though she shot her husband, she seems an unlikely suspect in the deaths of Al Sweetner and her son Stanley. In the hospital morgue Archer learns that Elizabeth Broadhurst's bullet did not kill Leo Broadhurst. Among his bones they find the broken tip of a butcher knife. However, the authorites refuse to discuss the case with Archer. When Kelsey tells him that word has come down to exclude him, the traditional split between the independent detective and the institutional authorities reemerges.

24) At the Broadhurst Ranch
Archer finds Brian Kilpatrick trying to take from Jean a briefcase of documents and Mrs. Broadhurst's pistols which he claims she wants at the hospital. Archer accuses Kilpatrick of blackmail and involvement in Leo Broadhurst's murder. Kilpatrick leaves, threatening to have Archer run out of town and subsequently we learn that he goes home and kills himself. As the truth emerges it pulls apart the festering irresponsible relationships and lays the groundwork for those who will face the truth to restore their relationships.

25) A Fifth Visit to Mrs. Snow's
Learning from the Los Angeles Police that Fritz bought the wig and beard, Archer goes to the Snow's house. Fritz says that the hair pieces were stolen and accuses his mother. Under Archer's questioning he remembers that she told him to bury Leo Broadhurst (see #21 above). Fritz explains that he followed Stanley to the Mountain House, saw him digging where his father was buried, and phoned Mrs. Snow. Fritz tells Archer that Al Sweetner called and talked to Mrs. Snow about money the night he was killed. Then Mrs. Snow gave Fritz a sleeping pill and presumably went out.

Archer accuses her of killing Al, Stanley, and Leo. She finally admits that she also went to the Mountain House that night fifteen years before, found Leo Broadhurst unconscious, stabbed him to death, and had Fritz bury him. She calls Leo, "a wicked man . . . a fornicator,"[47] and blames him for Fritz's trouble with the law. Since then she has been paying off Al Sweetner just as Mrs. Broadhurst has been paying off Brian Kilpatrick. When Archer calls the police she attempts to knife him but Archer overpowers her.

26) The Return Home
In many ways the novel closes as it opens. Archer, Ronny, and Jean drive home with the boy in the middle. The secrets of the past maintained a facade of normalcy but for fifteen years the irresponsible selves who maintained those secrets denied themselves and others the possiblity of living in responsible relationship to each other.

Leo Broadhurst, the original underground man, poisoned all his relationships. His infidelity to his wife Elizabeth, to Ellen Strome Kilpatrick, and to Marty Knickerson affected each of their marriages - it destroyed his own to Elizabeth, and Ellen's to Brian Kilpatrick, and caused Marty's marriage to Lester Crandall (who accepted Broadhurst's child, Sue.) But the effect of these unresolved relationships does not end with Leo's death. It is visited on their children: Stanley, Sue, and Jerry. Finally the past reaches out to destroy Stanley and threatens his son Ronny.

Unfaithfulness, both sexual and personal, seems almost the greater sin than murder in The Underground Man. But it leads to murder, which must be the ultimate violation of relationship. Brian Kilpatrick and Mrs. Snow, who conspired in Leo's murder, are twisted by their crimes in ways which affect their children, Jerry and Fritz.

In the end the one murder, Leo's, leads after fifteen years to a second, Stanley's. Stanley's burial on top of his father's unmarked grave gives the tale an obvious underground man who masks another, deeper, underground man. The hope of the killers is that one crime will cover up another, but in Macdonald's world past and present are linked and the very acts which are intended to hide the past ultimately point to it. Only resolution of the past makes possible the resolution and restoration of

---

[47]Macdonald, The Underground Man, p. 248.

the relationships of the present. This restoration does not come easily, and by the time all the secrets are revealed Al Sweetner and Brian Kilpatrick are also dead, Elizabeth Broadhurst has had a heart attack, and Jerry, Sue, and possibly Ronny have been deeply scarred.

But resolution and restoration are possible. In Sausalito Jerry Kilpatrick is tentatively getting to know his mother. Sue is home, if in need of therapeutic help. And Fritz is freed of his mother's domination to face, perhaps too late, the possiblity of living as an adult. The most hopeful restoration is the return of Ronny to his mother. Perhaps the exploration of past secrets, the recognition of the web which bound them all, has freed the boy to live in the present.

3) Conclusions

It is not surprising that the detective story can be shown to reflect an ethical stance. A fiction which concerns itself with the revelation of wrong can hardly fail to engage the questions of the moral life.

While concern with the moral life is obvious in the mystery tale, traditional ethical structures do not provide a satisfactory guide to The Underground Man, or, I suspect, to the mystery tale in general.

Niebuhr suggests three possible questions with which one can respond to the moral query, "what shall I do?" Ontological ethics asks "what is my goal or ideal?" Deontological ethics asks "what is the law of my life?" And responsible ethics asks "what is going on?"

Ontological ethics, which emphasize goals and the image of the human as maker, do not seem to be the primary source of moral guidance for Archer.[48]

---

[48]Archer does have goals in the sense of overarching ideals - to bring about justice, to encourage positive family relationships, to assist youth to become mature adults. This principle is particularly revealed in his opportunities for sexual relationships. Almost always a higher moral law (having usually to do with a sense of responsibility

82

The detective seems constantly diverted from his goal by the ever widening pool of relationships and there is no closing clarity about what has been accomplished (made) at the final reuniting of the missing boy, his mother, and the detective.

Neither does deontology, with its emphasis on the search for the primal rule, seem to shape the tale.[49] The civil law is almost irrelevent to the plot, with all the villains, except Mrs. Snow, already dead by the time the police enter the tale. Archer's loyalty is not given first to any obvious rule but emerges as he responds in relationship to others.

What we find throughout The Underground Man is a modeling of responsible relationship by Archer, an exploration of the difficulties of so living, and the price of the failure to do so.

The question of responsiblity reveals and emphasizes the relationships in Macdonald's fiction. Archer's method is to follow the pathway of the disruption of these relationships to the events in the past which are the root of the current crisis. The question of responsibility leads to a reading of the tale as an examination of family life and conflict. Given what we know of Macdonald's self-understanding, these are questions the author himself would have affirmed.

Archer's struggle with his responsiblity to those at the margins of the tale - such as Elegant, Fritz Snow, and Jerry Kilpatrick - hints at his connection to a community broader than that of his clients. And that connection links his world to ours and thus suggests that his struggle with

toward the other) causes him to forsake the affair. As noted earlier both ontoligical and deontological ethics are at work within responsibility.

[49]Although he sometimes violates them, Archer does follow common rules of social and moral conduct - he is, by-and-large, a Ten Commandments guy. The important thing for the arguement developed here is that Archer functions primarily on the basis of resposible ethics.

complex problems of truly responsible (monotheistic) relationship is paralleled in the world.

However, the critic's task is not simply to measure the protagonist against some external standard of morality. Archer is, after all, a fictional character who, moral or immoral, must be considered a part of the totality of the fiction. The critic must ask: Does the image of responsibility reveal the text as a narrative whole? Do ethical questions shape the story? And what assumptions about the world (real or fictional) do these questions reveal? Simply put, our central question is whether The Underground Man may be said to be about the moral life as defined by the symbol of responsibility, and what asking that question reveals about the text.

The actions of no single character can answer these questions. Archer, in his interactions, is but one piece of the total mosaic of The Underground Man. From this mosaic a total picture of interaction emerges.

There is Leo Broadhurst, who represents a polytheistic separation of his various involvements. In his hedonism Leo is concerned only with his own pleasures. He is not then, in Niebuhr's terms, in relationship with any of those with whom he interacts. And Leo fails to see that what happens in one "dialogue" or interaction impacts the other and thus accepts his multiple sexual affairs.

But others are affected by Leo's actions and by his death. The tale may be seen as an exploration of the impact of the various ethics at work. His wife, denied a place in the present, turns back to the past with a morbid fascination with her father's life and her social position. The distorted moralisms with which Mrs. Snow defends her actions ("He was . . . a fornicator") present a twisted image of deontology's emphasis on law. Brian Kilpatrick and Al Sweetner present an equally negative image of how goals may be twisted.

A generation after Leo's death those involved in the murder (Elizabeth Broadhurst, Mrs. Snow, and Brian Kilpatrick) and those affected by it (Stanley, Marty Knickerson Crandall, Ellen Storm [nee Strome Kilpatrick], and Al Sweetner) continue to be affected by what happened. And a third generation (Ronny Broadhurst, Sue Crandall, and Jerry Kilpatrick) are drawn into the web of the past. As they face the question "what shall I do?," no clarification of goals or rules will help them. What we see in The Underground Man, as in the entire body of Macdonald's work, is the insistence that only the question "what is going on?," has the potential to break the bonds of the past and enable renewed life in the present and ongoing relationship in the future.

It is here that Niebuhr's ethic of responsibility raises the greatest questions about Macdonald's fiction, for Niebuhr suggests that responsibility is known in loyalty to some community, and monotheistic responsibility rests on loyalty to the community of being itself. The concept of responsibility does seem to shape the ethical discourse of the Archer novels. And the ethical standard which underlies the responsible dialogue of the tales is not simply that of the society in which they take place. But it is not clear what community upholds Archer in his decisions or what ultimate value it is to which the detective gives his loyalty.

Our reading suggests that the concern with responsiblity as an ethical demand, which Niebuhr argued was central to the modern discussion of the moral life, shapes Macdonald's tale. The problem at the root of the mystery grows out of the compounding of irresponsible relationships and the hiding of those relationships from the scrutiny of those who are affected by them. As we have seen, Leo Broadhurst's irresponsible relationships with women are at the heart of the problem, and they in turn create an ever widening circle of irresponsible relationships that come to affect his children and his children's children.

One thing which keeps Macdonald's literary work from being simply an illustration of Niebuhr's ethic is the absence of a lasting religious community for Archer or any other character. For H. Richard Niebuhr the church serves as the embodiment of that present and historical community to which the self must be responsible. Because of this Niebuhr's responsible self is less alone than Macdonald's. But Niebuhr does not argue that responsibility is a uniquely Christian concern; rather he sees responsibility as the concept which shapes most of the modern discussion of the moral life. So it should be clear that neither he nor the author of this examination argue that only Christians behave responsibly. What Niebuhr does argue is that responsibility takes place within a community to which loyalty to being itself is the highest form of the responsible life.

Archer seems to have virtually no lasting community to which he can give his loyalty. The San Francisco detective, Willie Mackay, seems a respected colleague but Archer remains professionally a loner rather than a part of a detective agency or community. Archer's only marriage failed. There is the relationshp with Ronny and the possiblity of a romantic involvement with Jean but the reader familiar with the Archer tales can hold little hope for a lasting relationship for Archer. His community seems to come in brief snatches during the few days that his cases typically last. Niebuhr argues that a self cut-off from some larger community inevitably serves the narrow interests of the present. Indeed, Archer may be somewhat guilty of that. Though he has a standard one might argue that he, in some ways, takes advantage of others for the sake of the obligation he feels to the victim and his client. But there is less of this than a careful reading of Niebuhr would lead one to expect.

Archer gives the appearance of being an ethical agnostic. He clings to the hope that there exists a community to which he can give his loyalty, but he is never able to give himself fully to any community. The detective's loyalty is a limited one, which seems to flirt with the possibility of loyalty to being itself. He has experimented, as a police officer, with loyalty to his own culture and found that an inadequate frame of moral reference. Within the framework of his cases he experiments with loyalty, tests the world and his clients to see if loyalty is possible. But his explorations uncover the failings of people and social institutions and reveal how untrustworthy is a human community. Thus there is a movement toward ultimacy in his committment to his client that is given generic expression in the convention of the hard-boiled detective refusing to be ordered off the case, but, though the detective's commitment may be to a broader understanding of the problem than the client possesses, this commitment is limited to the solution of the particular problem the client faces and never seems to build to a lasting community. For Archer, as for so many of his generic compatriots, this inability to make lasting commitments is demonstrated by the failure of his marriage.

In _The Underground Man_ this experiment with loyalty can be seen in Archer's relations with Ronny and Jean Broadhurst. Archer expresses no interest when she asks if it is true that he is a detective, saying, "Yes, but this is my day off. I hope."[50] Along with his repression of his sexual interest in Jean, this professional disinterest serves to clarify that it is not self-interest, as commonly understood, that leads the detective to agree to look for Ronny Broadhurst. It is loyalty to the boy with whom he has established a tenuous link, and what that loyalty says about himself, that is Archer's primary motivation. Those first links lead to responsible dialogue with others, notably Sue Crandall. Though one wishes for some greater articulation on the detective's part about his values or motivations there is a hint of loyalty to something like "the one beyond the many" in Archer's behavior. But none of those committments proves to be lasting. And the unwillingness to pursue a relationship with Jean Broadhurst may be as much an expression of Archer's unwillingness to make again the long-term commitments of marriage as of Archer's focus on his commitment to her son. The detective remains suspicious of the life of human community. A fundamental conflict between his ideals and the society in which he lives leaves him unable to give himself to any ongoing commitment.

Niebuhr's _Christ and Culture_ helps us to understand why this split between the detective's values and society takes the form that it does. _Christ and Culture_ explores, from a Christian perspective, that relationship of people's ultimate loyalties to the culture in which they live. Niebuhr suggests that the problem of how to relate the ultimate demands of faith to the particular demands of a culture has always confronted believers and identifies five different ways in which the faithful have attempted to resolve this dialectic.

Followers of the _Christ against Culture_ model attempt a wholly spiritualized existence unshaped by cultural demand, while adherents of the _Christ of Culture_ model identify the demands of the culture

---

[50]Macdonald, _The Underground Man_, p. 5.

with those of the Christ. Niebuhr charges that both of these attempt to collapse the dialectic of faith by absolutizing some specific cultural value.

Niebuhr offers three mediating models which recognize the difference between ultimate and specific demands and attempt to relate them. The Christ above Culture model looks something like the second (Christ of Culture) but recognizes a realm apart from the cultural wherein the ultimate comes to bear. Christ and Culture in Paradox sees that the ultimate and the specific make simultaneous and conflicting demands which cannot be resolved. Finally, Christ the Transformer of Culture recognizes the conflicts between the two but believes that the ultimate is at work in the specific and has the power to transform it.

Archer makes no Christian confession, yet he seems to recognize an ultimate demand upon his life, and it may be that Niebuhr's typology can help us to understand the detective, the fiction in which he exists, and its relationship to the question of responsiblitly within a particular cultural setting.

Clearly the detective is no follower of any "Christ" of Culture. If he were, he would happily have remained a police officer. It is tempting, in the face of his discomfort with the culture in which he finds himself, to see him as a follower of some "Christ" against Culture. But if this were the case, Archer would withdraw from society even more fully and take none of the cases that continually draw him into involvement with the world.

Though deeply alienated from it, Archer is in the particular expression of the world which is his culture, and yet he is the servant of a demand which is not that of his culture, and so it must be through one of the mediating positions that Archer is understood. The Christ above Culture is of little use here because the conflicts Archer experiences are clearly in relationship to the world. And yet, though he engages the world's failure to conform to the ultimate, he lacks the conviction that the world can be fundamentally changed that marks the follower of the Transformer of Culture.

It is only with the model which recognizes the irresolvable conflict between ultimate and specific demands that we begin to get some hint of Archer's character. Were he a Christian, Archer would be an adherent to the Christ and Culture in Paradox model - living "precariously and sinfully in the hope of a justification which lies beyond history."[51]

Here we come up against the limits imposed by the absence of a clear monotheism which could value everything that is and critique every demand. And yet this should not surprise us. For while we might identify clearly Christian popular culture (especially of the Christ of Culture motif) we should hardly expect to find any genuinely monotheistic popular culture since it would, by nature, be at odds with the interests of society.[52] If the ultimate demand to which Archer is loyal were more clearly defined, its conflict with society would be clearer and the paradoxical nature of life in the world would be even more confrontationally raised.

Within the tales, society, both in the form of small boys and belligerent policemen, continues to make demands on the detective's loyalty, which Archer recognizes. And at times those demands are at odds with a larger loyalty which he also recognizes. In the absence of a clearly monotheistic commitment, this larger loyalty is not quite to being, itself. Loyalty to being, itself, is the ideal with which the detective flirts, toward which he moves and urges others, but to which he cannot fully give himself. And so the detective keeps his distance until such a time as ultimate loyalty is demanded of him within definable few day limits.

Taken as a whole, The Underground Man explores the ethic of responsibility. And the narrative seems to suggest that only such an ethic makes possible a resolution of the past which will allow for ongoing dialogue in the future. In the end, Ronny, Sue, and Jerry are reunited with their mothers. In order to accomplish this reuniting, Archer has had to break the narrow definitions of community and take a tentative step toward dealing with each of them as part of

---

[51]Niebuhr, Christ and Culture, p. 45.

[52]See Chapters Four for a discussion of the limits on the ability of popular culture to critique the society within which it functions.

the community of being itself. But in the end, because there is no community of the faithful to sustain him, Archer withdraws again to his lonely existence.

In the next chapter we will see why it is unlikely that a popular art form will directly confront the implications of the ultimate values hinted at here and force the reader to confront the paradoxical relationship between the demands of ultimate and specific loyalties, and how much less likely it is that, recognizing the two realms which must be mediated, hard-boiled detective fiction will give expression to a transformative ethic.

CONCLUSIONS:
THE SOCIAL AND ETHICAL IMPLICATIONS
OF THE ARCHER TALES

Before drawing conclusions, it is well to review some assumptions which underlie the present study. Throughout this book the goal has been to understand and describe the cultural patterns which exist in the texts and their relationship to the audience. In this descriptive approach, Macdonald's work is analyzed as a part of popular moral discourse, but it is not measured against any assumed moral norm. Throughout, the underlying question has been what is going on, rather than, what should be going on. From this study the implications, including ethical implications, of certain cultural patterns become clear, but no program for the reform of popular culture is implied or intended.

Macdonald's work is examined as an example of a popular genre. The ways in which it is like other popular tales are as important as the ways in which it is unique. It is in understanding both of these that the text's place in society can be understood. Given this approach the conclusions about the Archer tales should be suggestive of the way that other tales within the hard-boiled genre function. Further, this work should raise questions useful in thinking about other popular genres.

Having considered, in earlier chapters, the generic context of Macdonald's work, and having used the perspectives of Sigmund Freud and H. Richard Niebuhr to give close attention to several of his novels, conclusions can be drawn about the Archer novels and their audience, and about their role in popular ethical discourse.

The Archer tales are examples of the hard-boiled tradition of detective writing which uniquely meet the needs of the intellectual class. The nature of the protaganist, the literary style of the novels, Macdonald's criticisms of society and human nature, the relation of Religion (or ultimate values) and Culture, and the protagonist's alienation are all

91

elements of Macdonald's work that appeal to an intellectual audience. These elements seem to challenge the society described and implicitly that of the reader. But, ironically, the individualism and existential nature of these criticisms tend to confirm the status quo by suggesting that fundamental social change is impossible or at least highly unlikely and by encouraging an individualistic ethic which allows the individual to stand apart from his or her world.

Through the expression of accepted values and the integration of the reader into society, popular culture serves the culture within which it exists. And if one shares Freud's sense of the difficulty of this integration and its importance for the maintenance of civilization this is a valuable process. But the price of these positive benefits is the inability to speak out against the failings of society in a way which might be genuinely transformational.

Even when Macdonald's novels express progressive attitudes, such as those about race and ecology, they tend to confirm the status quo. This becomes evident when the following are considered: 1) the role of the individual in society, 2) the conservative nature of popular culture in general, 3) the focus on the individual within the tales, 4) the absence of a monotheistic critique of society, and 5) the way that the Archer tales function as a popular fiction for the intellectual class.

1) The Individual in Society

Macdonald's Lew Archer tales are, in keeping with hard-boiled convention, located in and around the cities of southern California. But more important than the specifics of their settings is the particular attitude toward the urban metropolis and what it suggests about human nature shared by writers of hard-boiled fiction. Understanding this attitude toward society is one of the places where Freud and Reinhold Niebuhr are helpful in thinking about the genre. The hard-boiled novel typically expresses a very Freudian attitude toward society. Reinhold

Niebuhr's discussion of the moral life[1] casts this tension within society in terms of the ethical conflict between the individual and society.

Like Freud, and unlike the Niebuhrs, the hard-boiled writers see people as driven strongly by an instinctual commitment to individual self-- interest. Freud suggests that society is valued for the restraint it imposes on others and for the advance which are possible only through cooperation. But society requires high levels of renunciation by individuals who accept the compromises demanded by civilization, if only because of the necessity of restraining their neighbors.[2] This world-view is seen clearly in the contrast between the hard-boiled and classical detective stories. The classical tale poses an orderly world[3] in which an exceptional, often upper class, individual is able to overcome some threat to that order. The hard-boiled protagonist is an ordinary, usually lower middle class, individual whose detective work reveals an underlying corruption in the world.

While, as we have seen, the hard-boiled tale focuses on the moral life of the individual, sin is presented as especially incarnate in group structures. Social institutions which ought to preserve a right relationship between individuals are corrupted by the self-interest of the individuals who control them. This is typically represented by the police. Macdonald also uses the medical

---

[1]See Chapter One.

[2]Both Freud and Reinhold Niebuhr describe this conflict between the individual and society. But where Reinhold Niebuhr sees this as an expression of the individual's moral superiority, Freud sees the conflict as an expression of the difficulty of restraining the individual ego.

[3]In applying Neibuhr's Christ and Culture motif to the classical tale one might explore the hypothesis that the classical detective story tends toward the Christ of Culture in its collapse of specific and ultimate loyalties.

profession[4] and the oil industry to demonstrate the corruptibility of human institutions. As we saw in Chapter One, the underlying conflict between the ethical standards that are possible for individuals and for institutions encourages a fundamental dishonesty about cultural self-interest and the institutions of society. The moral individual is repelled by the dishonesty inherent in society's defense of its pursuit of its own interests and thus sin is more likely than grace to be embodied in societal structures.

The difficulties of living in society are made worse by social inequalities. Society demands renunciation of every member of society but distributes the rewards for this renunciation unequally. This is given expression in The Moving Target in the presentation of Sampson's servants and particularly Albert Graves' treatment of them.

In order to function in society, individuals must balance the demands of their individual instinctual desires with the demands of society for restraint, respect for others, and cooperation. The novels portray the difficulty of this balance and Archer leads others to confront the imbalance in their lives and moves them, by encouragement or restraint, in the direction of that balance.

2) The Conservative Nature of Popular Culture

In a world in which it is difficult to balance the demands of society and individual desires, popular culture serves a conserving or maintenance function for society. By integrating inevitable changes in social patterns and values into existing fantasies, popular culture eases the adjustment of society to inevitable changes in attitudes and patterns and minimizes the conflict between emerging and established values. Popular culture works to maintain the existing order. Further, by offering aesthetic satisfactions that help to compensate for society's failings, popular culture helps to limit challenges to the structures of social life. This process is likely to encourage

---

[4]Criticism of the medical profession combines the criticim of institutions with the genre's antipathy for the wealthy.

an attitude toward society similar to that described by H. Richard Niebuhr with the Christ _of_ Culture model. The confirmation of societal values and attitudes in combination with the denial of any conflict within those values and attitudes tends to encourage the confusion of the specific (cultural, henotheistic) with the ultimate (monotheistic) demand.

Given the unequal distribution of social rewards, and the inevitable dissatisfaction of individuals who put their own interests ahead of those of others, unhappiness is inevitable in society. As Freud suggests[5] this dissatisfaction leads to erotic and ambitious wishes. These wishes are a potential threat to society in that they lead to alienation and may encourage individuals to act in antisocial ways to achieve the things they wish for.

By displacing the individual's wishes, popular culture allows people to enter into a shared fantasy life which provides the illusion of powers and freedoms that the audience desires but lacks. Where a privatized fantasy or day-dream alienates the individual, a shared fantasy reveals shared wishes and integrates the individual into society.

In an unjust society, and both Freud and Niebuhr see human society as inevitably imperfect and to varying degrees unjust, popular culture serves the purpose of maintaining the existing social order and justifying its inequalities. Given the difficulties the individual faces in submitting to society this is a necessary process if society is to be maintained.

The argument made here is not moral. It is not claimed that popular narrative is "good" or "bad" because it serves a particular social function; it is simply noted that the narrative serves to preserve society and minimize the tensions within society. This may not be a step in the direction of psychological or political advance. Norman Holland's insistence is well taken that "there is no guarantee that a

---

[5]See the discussion of Freud's essay "Creative Writers and Day-Dreaming" in Chapter Two.

plot . . . moves in the direction of maturation."[6]
In fact, based on the analysis in this study, one
function of a popular tale in an imperfect society
will be to confirm and maintain existing relationships
of inequality.

3) The Focus on the Individual

An important element in the conservatism of
the hard-boiled detective story is its affirmation
of individualism. The moral and psychological focus
of the tale is on the implication of the choices
that the individual makes in living in a less-than-ideal
world. H. Richard Niebuhr's stress on relationalism
helps us to see that the individualism of the
hard-boiled detective story protects the existing
interests of society by redirecting moral energy
away from social reform.

The hard-boiled detective is often forced to
confront the corruption of society, the fallenness
of the world. But with rare exceptions[7] the result
of that confrontation is not social change but confirmation, or salvation, of the moral character of the
individual. This individualistic ethic makes difficult
if not impossible the compromises that might lead
to coalitions for significant social change.

As was argued in Chapter One, the hard-boiled
detective's alienation from the world implies a
criticism of society which is a part of the tale's
appeal. But because, in Macdonald's world view,
corruption is inherent in human nature, and because
there is no community of monotheistic believers who
share Archer's moral standard, Macdonald's criticism
takes a form more like that of H. Richard Niebuhr's
Religion and Culture in Paradox model than Religion
the Transformer of Culture. In the hard-boiled
detective story the goal of the moral life is not

---

[6]Holland, The Dynamics of Literary Response
(New York: W.W. Norton & Co., 1975), p. 105.

[7]One example of a hard-boiled tale in which
the possiblity of real political reform is considered
is Dashiell Hammett's Red Harvest (New York:
Alfred A. Knopf, 1929).

to change the world but to stand sufficiently apart from it to function responsibly within it. By presenting in fantasy a hero who is able to live within a society from which he experiences alienation, these tales serve the ironic function of integrating the alienated reader into society.

Reinhold Niebuhur argues[8] that there is an inevitable conflict between what is morally possible for the individual and for society. This leads to a fundamental dishonesty in which, in order to ease the discomfort of the sensitive individual conscience, societies convince themselves of the beneficence of their own self-interest.

The hard-boiled detective story offers an alternative dishonesty that serves the same end - the integration of the individual into society. That is, it allows the individual to identify in fantasy with a protagonist who is presented as being in the world but not of the world. Such a fantasy allows the audience to imagine that, like the fictional detective, they see the corruption of society and, being true to a personal code, stand apart from society and are thus absolved of responsibility for society's failings. The result of this is to protect society from change in two ways: first, by suggesting that the nature of humanity and society is such that social reform is impossible, and secondly, by confirming the assumption that morality is really a matter of the behavior of individuals.

Ross Macdonald's use of psychology develops this generic convention. His interest is in individual psychology, his own as well as that of his characters, rather than the psychology of mass society. He is, for example, more likely to examine particular broken marriages than the larger social contract on which marriage rests. These interests are in line with the social purpose of the genre for they suggest that transformation is personal rather than social.

Imagine a reader whose sense of his or her own sophistication is rewarded by a fiction which recognizes the culture's dishonesty with itself, and who may

---

[8]See the discussion of Reinhold Niebuhr's Moral Man and Immoral Society in Chapter One.

experience some degree of alienation from society, but who nonetheless has made a reasonably comfortable place in the world. That is, think of a member of the intellectual class. As we shall see subsequently, Macdonald's fiction functions in a number of ways to serve the needs of such a reader. For now it is enough to recognize that members of the intellectual class have a highly developed sense of individualism which makes the individualism of the genre appealing. The result of Macdonald's emphasis on individual psychology within an already individualistic genre is an appealing fantasy which shares the reader's focus on the individual and seems to criticize the reader's world but presents no real threat to it.

4) The Absence of Monotheism

Using H. Richard Niebuhr's concept of the responsible self to examine The Underground Man helps us to see the nature of the ethical discourse in Macdonald's world. But attention to Niebuhr also draws our attention to the absence of any satisfactory monotheistic expression in the Archer tales. The specifics of particular social and personal interactions are criticized in the novels, and there is, as we have seen with Macdonald's presentation of wealth and especially of the oil industry, an implicit criticism of broader social structures. But nowhere in considering the demands upon the self is there the recognition of what Niebuhr called "the One beyond the many," no clear loyalty to "being itself."

It may well be that no genuinely monotheistic tale could achieve popularity with a mass audience. A monothestic stance inevitably challenges the conventions of any particular society, and thus dis-integrates the reader from that society. Because both society and the individual need this process of social confirmation and integration, it is unlikely that large numbers of people would find satisfaction in tales which genuinely challenge their place in the world they know.

Even a fiction like Macdonald's, which we have seen to be concerned with responsibility, limits the community of obligation and it is precisely this limitation which enables the Archer tales to find a mass audience. That there is a limit to that community does not make the reflection on responsibility valueless to the individual or to society. But Archer's responsible interaction should not be confused with a truly monotheistic stance, and the critic who wishes to understand the social function of the tales must recognize that limitation.

Just as Macdonald's doctrine of God, or his lack of a clear one, adds to the tendency to accept the present order, so does his doctrine of humanity. Where fallenness, by what ever name it may be known, is taken as seriously as it is by Macdonald, it tends to limit criticism of society since the doctrine holds little hope for the transformation of a society made by human hands.

Clearly the author of popular fiction has no obligation to portray responsibility in monotheistic terms. But the critic must recognize the limits of the popular genre within which Macdonald chose to work. In the hard-boiled detective tale social criticism is possible, but that criticism is constrained by the form of the tales and the function of popular culture.

The result is a criticism which gives expression to dissatisfactions within society in a way that does not call for fundamental change in society but in fact helps to integrate the dissatisfied into society. Macdonald's work, as a particularly sophisticated form of popular culture, expresses an existential awareness of what is wrong. But, as has been repeatedly observed, the genre's apparently harsh criticisms of society are not accompanied by any program for change. Indeed the tales suggest that human nature itself will prevent any substantive change. And thus ethics becomes a matter of individual standards and morality. Such an ethical system accepts society as it exists.

Given this absence of a clear monotheistic standard against which to measure society, and without a theological or sociological understanding of the human situation which sees transformation as a real possibility, Macdonald's fiction falls into social and generic patterns which limit the ability of its criticisms to genuinely be a voice for significant social change. When one is aware of this pattern in popular culture, and the function it serves, the problem in analyzing Macdonald's fiction is clearly to understand why it gives expression to dissatisfactions with society at all and why it is that these particular dissatisfactions surface in the way they do.

5) A Popular Fiction for the Intellectual Class

Our understanding of a popular fiction and its cultural function is sharpened by a consideration of who makes up its audience and the audience's place in society. This may be especially helpful where the audience for a particular author differs from that for the genre as a whole.

Ross Macdonald writes within a popular tradition that has received minimal critical and academic attention. As was suggested in Chapter One the genre was developed in the United States by writers influenced both by the classical British detective story and the American action-adventure formulas. In that process the typically upper class, often amateur, protagonist of the clasical tale was replaced by a lower middle class professional who was likely to be abrasive, even crude, and less obviously aligned with the social order than his English predecessor. The audience for this genre has its roots in the blue collar pulp magazines where the genre was developed.

The assumption that, as intellectuals, academics and critics stand apart from and above mass society has interfered with the critical examination of the hard-boiled detective story. One's status as an intellectual is challenged by the confession of serious interest in popular works and when the intellectual turns his or her attention to those works, the intellectual's traditions encourage skeptical evaluation of the worth of the popular novel.

Given the lack of critical attention typically given to the detective story, it is noteworthy that Ross Macdonald has been singled out from among the writers of hard-boiled fiction for particular attention and acclaim by critics and scholars. Attention should be given to what makes Macdonald's Lew Archer tales particularly satisfactory to the intellectual class.

In explaining Macdonald's appeal, emphasis has typically been placed on Macdonald's literary accomplishment, that is, his erudition, style, and especially his command of simile. But in the absence of a clear transformational critique of society, these literary skills serve to tell a story in which displaced wish fulfillment and the exploration and resolution of particular psychic and social tensions combine to integrate the intellectual into society.

Freud regards popular fiction as a shared fantasy, the primary function of which is wish fulfillment. He further suggests that wishes may be typed as ambitious and erotic and that the wish is the result of unhappiness over satisfactions that we lack. Archer is a hard-boiled hero aligned with the interests of an intellectual audience and the story of his cases offers, in fantasy, compensation for the unhappinesses of the intellectual class.

As a class, intellectuals have a unique place in society. In pursuit of the aesthetic path to happiness, they renounce the most direct stisfaction of erotic and ambitious desires. And it appears to the intellectual that the renunciations to which he or she submits are not equally shared by other classes. The upper class seems, to the intellectual, free to pursue ambitious satisfactions and the lower classes seem to be free from social and ethical constraints to pursue erotic satisfactions. In return for his or her renunciations, the intellectual receives aesthetic satisfactions that are little understood or appreciated by others.

Like the intellectual, Archer is committed to the authority of the rational. While he has a satisfying physical competence, analysis and evaluation are the skills more likely to lead to the resolution of his cases. A fiction that makes use of the settings of tales of action and adventure but that grants ultimate authority to the rational mind has great appeal to intellectuals in a culture which affirms the life of action. A fantasy in which an action hero, who can be seen as a displacement of the reader, acts with power and authority while using the gifts of the intellectual has obvious appeal to the intellectual class.

Archer goes among all classes and seems to have considered the conventional satisfactions of each and chosen to share the renunciations of the intellectual. But within the fantasy he is respected by those whose choices are different from his own, and he is thus affirmed as a wise man who can serve as a model for others.

A return to H. Richard Niebuhr's ethical model draws our attention to certain implications of the social adaptation of the intellectual, as it is facilitated by Macdonald's fiction, which would not be evident without the cross-disciplinary approach taken here.

The ethical position so appealing to the intellectual class, which Macdonald expresses in his fiction, is one which approximates that of Niebuhr's Religion and Culture in Paradox. Those who hold this dualist position do not confuse the demand of the ultimate with that of a specific culture, nor do they think that it is possible to live outside of the demands of culture, but they also do not think that the ultimate can finally and fundamentally transform culture. Because of the seriousness with which the sinful nature of human culture is taken such persons experience a paradox between the demands of their culture and a wider community (ultimately that of being itself) which they regard as inescapable. In this system of ethical thought culture does come under the judgment of the ultimate, but it is not thought possible to make society perfect.

Macdonald's fiction reveals an important social result of this ethical understanding. In Archer's statements and actions the limitations of society are exposed and judged, but no hope is held out for a transformation of society. And in the place of the hope of social transformation is the individualist ethic which drives the detective to the edge of a society which he is not wholly a part of, but which he cannot escape.

For the individual, a Religion and Culture in Paradox stance enables life in society which takes seriously the critique of society implicit in ultimate values which are not identical to the value of society. But, how is society served by a fiction that points out this conflict in values between the individual and society itself? Society is served by a stance which integrates a marginalized group into society by limiting their expectation of social change and encouraging the attitude that ultimate values have primarily to do with the actions and attitudes of the individual.

Raising these social questions implies a critique of the Religion and Culture in Paradox position.

While it is intellectually clearly distinct from that of the Religion _of_ Culture, when it comes to action aimed at changing society, there seems to be little functional difference between the two. While the Religion of Culture perspective overtly affirms the ultimacy of the values of society, the Religion and Culture in Paradox position diffuses criticism of society by its implicit assumption that, bad as it may be, society can be little improved. Ultimate values become personalized and criticize society without calling for change. While they may tend to function for different classes, the two positions serve to integrate the individual into society in a way which preserves existing social relationships.

This social integration is a process which intellectuals need at least as much as others. And, recognizing the combination of aesthetic, ethical, psychological, and social patterns within Ross Macdonald's work, it is not surprising that Macdonald has been accepted by intellectuals as their own writer of hard-boiled fiction. The Archer tales not only meet their aesthetic expectations but affirm their values and orientation to society while satisfying in fantasy their dissatisfactions.

APPENDIX
FROM NOVEL TO FILM

When, as in this study, our attention is drawn
to the same tale presented as a novel and a film,
the differences between the two media are highlighted.
To understand the changes made in the tale in the
adaptive process we must consider the properties
and conventions of both media.[1] The literary form
communicates almost exclusively through language,
the cinematic art form principally through visual
images and dialogue. Literature is, thus, an easier
medium in which to present internal experience than
film, which can more easily express external, physical
experience. This is not to say that a novel cannot
portray action or a film emotion. But in the film
physical action and dialogue give outward expression
of the internal thoughts or emotions of a character
while the novelist is free to express the character's
inner experience directly. In a film, external action
points to internal experience. Thus, sorrow might
be expressed on the screen by an extreme close-up
showing the path of a tear.

1) Two Narrative Arts

Literature and the cinema are quite different
media dependent on different means of communication.
Yet, Bluestone points out that "both pre-suppose
a spectator"[2] and Eisenstein suggests that as far
as audience motivation is concerned, the novel and
film have few differences, i.e., the audience is

---

[1]The progression is usually from novel to
film though there is also a tradition of adaptation
of film to novel, some of which have even become
bestsellers, as is the case with Kotzwinkle's ET.

[2]George Bluestone, Novels Into Film (Berkeley:
University of California Press, 1957), p. 8.

always interested in a 'good story' regardless of its medium of communication.[3] We have then an object (the tale) and a subject (the audience) and our attention is drawn to both. Though the use made of the medium clearly matters to the audience, Eisenstein is correct in insisting that the audience's pleasure is rooted primarily in the experience of the tale itself, rather than in the nature of the medium[4] through which the tale is told. One evidence of this is the existence of an audience for specific genres, such as the mystery tale, in such diverse media as print, theatre, radio, television, and film.

As we shall see, the differences in the properties of the two media, in combination with the differences of their social and historical context, make narrative difference inevitable. For those who know and value one text before their exposure to the other, it is often difficult to look dispassionately at the differences. There is a strong tendency to regard changes from the text we first experienced as tampering, rather than as potentially interesting variations growing out of the nature of the two media. O'Toole complains,

> adaption challenges a battery of preconceptions even as they assault our memories. If a movie tells us that Hardy's Tess looks and moves the way Nastassia Kinski does, there's not a damn thing we can do about it.[5]

---

[3]*Film and Form*, as cited by William Crouch, "Satanism and Possession in Selected Contemporary Novels and Their Cinematic Adaptions" (unpublished Ph.D. dissertation, Department of Radio, TV, and Film, Northwestern University, 1976), p. 3.

[4]Though the audience's attention is usually focused on the tale, there is no experience of the tale separate from its presentation through some medium of expression.

[5]Lawrence O'Toole, "Now Read the Movie," *Film Comment*, November/December 1982, pp.34-38.

I suspect that the respective social positions of film and of what is thought of as serious literature, and of their respective audiences, is a source of much of this discomfort with the process of adaption. With the possible exception of films based on immensely popular best sellers, a film serves as a popularizer of the novel's tale. Thus, some of our discomfort with the changes doubtless grows out of our assumption of the purity of the culturally affirmed "high art" literary text. It may be that while the same critical issues are present in any literature-to-film adaptation, an adaptation of a "popular" or "low art" novel presents fewer cultural issues. One wonders if the critic would be less critical of the observation that, "If a movie tells us that Macdonald's Lew Archer looks and moves like Paul Newman or Spillane's Mike Hammer like Armand Assante, there is nothing we can do about it." It may be the popularization of the respected work that causes a problem rather than the specificity of the visual image.

There is a long history of the movies drawing on and influencing popular literature in genres such as the western, the horror tale, and melodrama. The detective story also has been presented in various media. The genre adaptation has a double advantage in the hard-boiled detective story for the action format lends itself to film adaption and there is less critical prejudice about the required changes. But it remains true that each medium has its own audience and conventions. Bluestone, for example, documents a tendency in his day for film to move toward romance and a happy ending.[6]

Some differences between novel and film are not explained as much by differences in form as by differences in audience and audience expectation. Bluestone links the development of the novel to the ascendency of the middle class. He finds the novel has "a complex but common body of themes, settings and attitudes which are characteristic of middle class refractions."[7] He contrasts this middle class audience with the much broader audience for the popular cinema.

---

[6]See Bluestone, p. 42.

[7]Ibid., p. 32.

The Novel

The novel is, of course, a longer work of prose fiction. But defining it beyond this general assertion becomes problematic. "Longer" is an elastic term and while one might suggest tentatively that a novel might be as short as 15,000 words or well in excess of 200,000 the American Heritage Dictionary settles for "of considerable length."[8] The existence of works like Norman Mailer's The Executioner's Song and Truman Capote's In Cold Blood suggests that "fiction" may be equally elastic.

These longer prose works usually are engaged by a single reader who controls the pace, and possibly even the sequence, of the narrative. The reader must bring to the work an acquired skill, the ability to translate abstract symbols (letters, words) into meaningful language patterns. While the individual experience of reading the novel is duplicated by many other people each reads independently, controlling the pace and even skipping some words. Also, the needed audience is small enough that novels can be written for quite specialized audiences.

It is not true, as some assume, that the literary art form gives us more information than the visual forms do. What is true is that they provide quite different kinds of information. Matters of physical setting such as lighting, objects, and the relationship between people and objects are not inherently literary and are made concrete only as the author chooses to describe them. For instance, the first chapter of Macdonald's The Underground Man takes place at Archer's apartment but we are told nothing about the apartment except that it is on the second floor and has a bedroom in which he awakens. It is an apartment, but nothing makes it a specific apartment except the assertion that it is Archer's. There is little more physical description of the courtyard where Archer first meets the Broadhursts. The information which the novel can give us, that a film cannot without interrupting the illusion of the medium, is interiority - a description of the

---

[8]American Heritage Dictionary (New York: Houghton Mifflin Company, 1969), p. 898.

specific inner response of the characters. This makes the first person narrative common in the hard-boiled detective story particularly difficult to duplicate. When, in that novel, Stanley Broadhurst leaves with Ronny, Archer reports, "The pang of fear I felt for the boy had become a nagging ache."[9] There are not visual equivalents for this emotional subjectivity of the narrator.[10]

Novel reading is the activity of an at least minimally educated individual. The formal qualities of the novel make it uniquely suited for expressing interior experience, and its historical development demonstrates that it is the middle class which has been most drawn to the art form uniquely expressive of the inner life.

Film

The illusion of moving pictures is believed to exist because of a physiological phenomenon known as persistence of vision. It is thought that the brain retains the image received by the eye for a brief instant. Therefore, a series of sequential pictures viewed rapidly gives the illusion of movement. This principle can be simply domonstrated by the once popular "flip book," in which the viewer flipped the pages from front to back so that, in a series of illustrations, a cartoon character seems to walk or wave. Similarly, the motion picture camera records a series of still photographs (normally 24 per second for a 35mm film) which when played back, give the

---

[9]Macdonald, The Underground Man, p. 6.

[10]Voice-over narration is one method of approximating internal information in a film. In 1946 Robert Montgomery directed and appeared in The Lady in the Lake, (based on Chandler's novel of the same title), an experiment with the use of subjective camera as a substitute for the literary technique of first person narration. The film is shot almost entirely from the perspective of the detective. While fascinating, the film highlights the problems of such an approach by drawing our attention to the differences between the way the camera and the eye see.

illusion of movement. This ability to perceive meaning and motion is an inherent rather than a learned activity. Thus we "read" the film image with little conscious effort just as we read objects and actions around us. This is different from the learned activity of reading, where we must recognize and consciously translate arbitrary symbols into words and phrases.

The edges of the screen may be thought of as a frame within which we see the film. The frame remains constant but within it the film maker presents a series of changing images. People, actions, and objects exist within a fragmented space, for while the frame remains constant, the camera's position and relation to that which it records is constantly changing so that the space contained within the frame varies. Time is similarly fragmented by elipsis and other manipulations of time and space.

Normally, in a modern film, sound is also recorded, manipulated, and presented with the visual image. Dialogue, music and aural effects are all added to the film, but they remain "Subsidiary to the moving image."[11] That is, they are correlative to the dominant visual material and are interpreted in relation to it. In the novel, dialogue stands alone, but in film, the spoken word exists simultaneously with a spatial image.

Interpreting this complex of images is complicated by the fact that much of the information provided by the film is not translated into words. All that is on the screen shapes our experience of the film, including much that the narrative does not focus our attention upon. Objects, the relationship of objects, their colors, lighting, movement and gesture, all add to and shape our interpretation of the tale. As was noted above, the apartment in Macdonald's The Underground Man remains undefined, but Archer's lodging in the made-for-TV film is a quite specific apartment in which objects (including an antique safe used as a wine rack and a W.C. Fields poster) do much to define the detective and his place in society. And Harper opens in the office where the detective has taken up residence. Here again, the specific furnishings and their disarray provide an

---

[11]Bluestone, p. 28.

unspoken commentary on the detective and the state
of his life and marriage.

Within a film, narrative attribution is somewhat
more complicated than in the novel. The problem
of the first person narrative explored by Robert
Montgomery in The Lady in the Lake has already been
noted. Film generally seems most similar to the
point of view of the third-person omniscient observer
of literature. But the visual point of view of a
film is constantly shifting and is sometimes directly
attributed to one of the characters within the film
in a point of view shot. Thus, while the tale may
appear to be told by a single character (who may
even function as narrator) the primary data will
usually include information as it was perceived by
various individuals, occasionally an omniscient observer
outside the tale (i.e., the viewer/film maker), but
usually a series of characters within the tale.
It may be helpful to think of this as two levels
of attribution, one roughly equivalent to the literary
narrator, the second an expression of the constantly
shifting visual point of view which is the masked
viewing point of the film maker. Writer-director
George Miller's The Road Warrior (1982) provides
an interesting example of this. The film opens and
closes with a voice over narrative which identifies
the tale as the elderly sounding narrator's memories
of long past events. Only at the end is that voice
identified with a particular character within the
film, the child played by Emil Minty. Thus, the
larger frame seems to be that of gradually identified
second person narrative. But the visual attribution
is not limited by this emerging voice. The child's
is but one of many visual points of view behind which
we finally find film maker George Miller. This process
masks the film maker's manipulation of the material
and adds to the impression that we are seeing a simple
record of reality; for if we ask from whose perspective
we see this, the film provides an answer within the
tale.

Beyond the internal issue of narrative attribution
is the surrounding question of authorship. Novels
are normally the product of a single artistic imag-
ination. A few trusted readers may make suggestions
before the novel is submitted for publication and
the editor at a publishing house may continue the
process. Occasionally a novel may be a collaboration
by several writers, such as the police procedurals
of Maj Sjowald and Per Wahloo, but in any case it

is the writer who is acknowledged as the artist. In film this becomes more complicated. Theories of film authorship have traditionally focused on the film director as the creative presence behind a film, but one might argue for the authorial stamp of particular producers, screenwriters, cinematographers, and actors. All feature films are collaborative art works shaped by many of those who worked on them. This is a fact of film production paralleled in other art forms like the theatre and the symphony which need not be seen as a negative unless one embraces the image of the singular artist as the only aesthetically pure road to creation.

The audience's relation to the film object is also different from its relation to literature. We usually view films in groups in a place and at a time set aside for that activity. Though the darkness of the theatre provides a kind of private reverie, the public nature of the experience is underscored by the possibility that the audience will respond with laughter, groans or applause. Who can imagine an individual applauding on completing a novel?

The pace at which we engage the film is also predetermined. The film unfolds at 24 frames a second and thus holds each viewer for the same amount of time. This unrelenting movement forward refuses the stop for the viewer who wishes to pause and reflect, or to re-experience a particular passage. While one with access to an editing table or videotape player may see the film alone and alter its speed, this is a limited control for we rapidly lose the illusion of movement on which the film rests if we slow the film very much. In any event, unlike novels, films are typically seen at a single sitting at a predetermined and unchanging pace.

Narrative film is a public art form which tells a tale by creating the image of the outward appearance of things. Usually viewed by groups, it communicates through the simultaneous presentation of complex visual and aural information which the audience intuitively identifies and interprets in relation to narrative and visual conventions.

2) Film as Popular Art

From its earliest days, film has been a narrative art form with a broad popular audience. The first audiences may have been delighted with any moving image - a train entering a station or a woman feeding a baby - but very quickly film began to tell stories. This tendency toward narrative encourages the comparison to literature, but other parallels may be more instructive. Bluestone suggests that film's roots are in the popular arts. He suggests that film-tragedy, film-comedy, and film-romance grow out of the discovery of filmic means of satisfying the working class audience rather than by "running away from the folk-art characteristics of the primative film."[12]

Bazin reminds us that "Cinema developed under sociological conditions very different from those in which the traditional arts exist."[13] Thus he suggests that it is not theatre and the novel which most influenced the cinema. Rather,

The first film-makers effectively extracted what was of use to them from the art with which they were about to win their public, namely the circus, the provincial theatre, and the music hall.[14]

---

[12]Bluestone, p. 7. What Bluestone calls a "folk art" would today be more accurately described as a popular art. The distinction is helpful for it differentiates between folk art created by people for their own consumption and the popular arts which exist in a market economy. While both may be described in terms of their conventions and explored in relation to the society which produced them, they are created under different constraints. The folk art is created within the community by an accessible artisan to satisfy a much more narrowly defined audience than the popular art. To be successful, the popular artist must satisfy a much broader audience with whom he or she has little direct contact.

[13]Andre Bazin, "In Defense of Mixed Cinema" in What is Cinema I, trans. Hugh Gray (Berkeley: University of California Press, 1967), p. 57.

[14]Ibid.

This search for the broadest possible audience seems inevitable, for film is an industrial art form which requires large sums of money to enable the work of many creative participants. A novel is usually written by a single individual and the direct costs are for paper and pen. While publishing is increasingly expensive, it costs little to prepare a manuscript for submission to a publisher and it is still possible to bring out a novel for a relatively small audience at a cost which is not prohibitive. But even a relatively simple film only begins with the writing. Producer, support crew, performers, and the film editor must be provided their expensive equipment and time to work before the film can be said to exist at all. For example, John Sayles' The Return of the Secaucus Seven (1980) is often cited as an example of extremely low budget film making which surprisingly found theatrical release. Yet Secaucas Seven is reported to have cost $60,000[15] and that figure apparently doesn't include eventual payments to participants after the film was released. Today a studio production with a budget of two or three million dollars is regarded as a low-budget film.

Films must reach a very broad audience if their costs are to be recovered and a profit shown. While this economic constraint may be regarded as a limit on the film artist, all art is created within particular limits. These economic limits on film making are a blessing to the student of popular culture, for the size of the audience needed to make such works economically viable suggests that when we understand the films and their relationship to their audience, we will learn not only about the interests of an individual author but about broader cultural patterns of meaning. Commenting on the role of the audience and the censor in shaping film narrative, Bluestone writes, "In film, more than any other arts, the signature of the social forces is evident in the final work."[16]

---

[15]See David Osborne, "John Sayles - From Hoboken to Hollywood - and Back," American Film, October 1982, pp. 31ff.

[16]Bluestone, p. 35.

In spite of their differences in form, literature and film are, particularly for the broad popular audience, narrative arts. And the process of adapting novels for the screen began early. This "adaptation" is inevitably problematic for, as Bluestone points out,

> An art whose limits depend on a moving image, mass audience, and industrial production is bound to differ from an art whose limits depend on language, a limited audience, and individual creation.[17]

What makes this process of adaptation problematic is the relationship between the two texts. The arts have long informed each other, but when poet Paul Carroll published his "Endless Ode to Oldenburg's Bat Column for Chicago"[18] the poem is understood to be inspired by, or as a commentary on, Claes Oldenburg's sculpture. When Orson Welles filmed _Othello_ (1952), a more direct connection was implied between Welles' and Shakespeare's texts. A discussion of their relationship requires an understanding of the differences in the two forms, the social context of the two media, and the historical situation in which the two texts were created. Further, the critic's assumptions about the adaptive process and the obligation (if any) of the adapter to find some equivalent expression which is faithful to the original text will enter in.

3) Adaptation

The process of adapting a novel for the screen requires a recognition of the difference in the two media. In order to adapt a novel into a film, it is necessary to discover the material phenomena which replaces the thought processes of the novel or to bypass the sequences of interiority.

In addition to the formal differences in the nature of the media, the successful adaptation takes into account the differences in the context of the

---

[17]_Ibid._, p. 64.

[18]_Chicago Magazine_, January, 1979.

two media. The confirmation of the audience's expectations of a popular art, the creative involvement of a large group in the production of the film, and the tendency of popular film to move toward generic norms, all reshape the narrative. Given these differences, paraphrase is the most we can hope for; direct equivalence is impossible in the narrative cinema.

This may seem to suggest that the film is inevitably a lesser work since it never lives up to the literary antecedent. But it must be remembered that just as the novel does some things which a film cannot, the reverse is also true. The film and novel are different experiences and each offers its own satisfactions. O'Toole points to this when he urges the reader to savor a passage from Hemingway's A Farewell to Arms for which he can imagine no visual equivalent and suggests that

> the transference of such a passage from page to sprocket is beyond likelihood. To that end too, no novel -- not even Bram Stroker's -- could give us [Werner] Herzog's Nosferatu walking across the town square, and the image, pausing to see if anyone is looking, and looking directly at us, and then walking out of the image to borrow blood of another kind.[19]

Giving the formal differences between the two media and their unique social contexts, what seems on the surface to be the same narrative in two forms is inevitably quite different. What the adaptive process gives us is variations on a narrative which must be as much appreciated for their unique qualities as for their ability to reproduce an experience from another medium.[20]

---

[19]O'Toole, Film Comment, November/December 1982, p. 38.

[20]The adaptive process is examined in Fiction into Film (New York: Dell, 1970). R. Maddux's novella A Walk in the Spring Rain is presented along with the S. Silliphant screenplay based on it and a commentary by N. D. Issacs highlighting the changes and unique qualities of the texts.

Adaptation presents both technical and critical problems. There is the practical issue of how the tale is transformed into a new medium and the question of how we shall think about the process.

Adaptation as a Technical Problem

Having recognized that differences in the two media make it impossible for film to duplicate our experience of a novel, we are left with film adaptations to evaluate. Bluestone writes:

> What happens, therefore, when the filmist undertakes the adaptation of a novel, given the inevitable mutation, is that he does not convert the novel at all. What he adapts is a kind of paraphrase of the novel - the novel viewed as raw material. He looks not to organic novel, whose language is inescapable from its theme, but to characters and incidents which have somehow detached themselves from language and, like the heroes of folk legends, have achieved a mythic life of their own.[21]

Bazin recognizes the same problem in his use of the term "equivalents" to describe the relationship between novel and film. But the French critic seems to seek a greater fidelity to the original than does Bluestone. He argues,

> It is wrong to present fidelity as if it were necessarily a negative enslavement to an alien aesthetic . . . the differences in aesthetic structure make the search for equivalents an even more delicate matter, and thus they require all the more power of invention and imagination from the film maker who is truly attempting a resemblance.[22]

The film maker must recreate the novel within a visual medium. Sometimes this will require the visual recreation of actions and events described in the novel. Or, in place of a direct equivalent

---

[21]Bluestone, p. 62.

[22]Bazin, p. 67.

for a scene in the novel the film maker may look for an indirect parallel in which deletions and additions to the narrative lead to a more complete equivalence.

The internal experience of the character must find its visual equivalent. And though this action may be distinctive, it is less specific than the literary description of interiority.

There is further complication in the way the two media use symbols. In a film, all objects on the screen are a part of an experience and affect our interpretation of the narrative. In a realistic presentation a symbolic object, such as the cross, has both an objective and a symbolic existence. Bluestone suggests that "almost any passage by Marcel Proust" will illustrate those literary images which

> . . . depend for their effect precisely on the fact that they are not to be taken literally . . . it is a way, then of packed symbolic thinking which is peculiar to imaginative thinking rather than visual activity.[23]

Proust may write of someone walking as if perched on giant stilts, but there is no"as if" in the cimema. If the analogy is made visually the stilts must exist. Therefore, the film maker must seek out some symbols but avoid others.

Adaptation as a Critical Issue

The middle-brow critical response to adaptation, such as that found in the film reviews presented in popular general interest magazines, has been generally negative. The fact that the film is not the same as the novel on which it was based has led many to reject it. Such criticism catalogues additions and deletions without considering the reasons for the changes. Assuming that the novel is the primary text, the film is treated as a simplification or distortion of the original. The problems with such a critical approach have already been indicated. To disapprove of the adaptation for failing to be what it cannot be, an exact

---

[23]Bluestone, p. 23.

118

substitute for the original, is to misunderstand the adaptive process. It is only by examing the subtle interplay of two unique texts, with the similarities and variations which grow out of their nature and context, that we can understand and appreciate the adaptation and its relationship to the tale in its original form.

More sophisticated critics have objected to the adaptation on the grounds that each of the arts should find its unique form and subject. Andre Bazin responds to this desire for a pure cinema with "In Defense of Mixed Cinema" where he argues that adaptions "are an established feature of the history of art."[24] Bazin's examples include the influence of Gothic sculpture on Renaissance painting, and preclassical tragedy's adaptation of the pastoral novel. After examining film's debt not only to the novel but to the popular theatrics of the circus and music hall, Bazin goes on to explore the medium's influence on novelists such as Graham Greene. Having argued that it is normal for the arts to draw on each other, Bazin concludes that

> to pretend that the adaptation of novels is a slothful exercise from which the true cinema, 'pure cinema,' can have nothing to gain, is critical nonsense to which all adaptions of quality give the lie.[25]

There have also been those who argue against the adaptation on the basis of its assumed impact on the literary work. Is the original well served by the changes inherent in the adaptive process? Certainly there are authors displeased with the adaptation of their work who would say no. But it would seem that what is usually criticized here is the popularization process, with literature being defended as a higher art form whose purity should be respected. An immediate response is that the original continues to exist and that, served well or poorly by its adaptation, remains unchanged in its original form. What may change is its audience

---

[24]Bazin, p. 56.

[25]Ibid., p. 68.

and the audience's assumptions about both author and text.

Bluestone argues that the adaptation increases the audience for the original and cites as evidence the practice of releasing special editions of the novel linked to the release of a film adaptation. O'Toole questions the value of this, pointing out that "Kids, who form the bulk of the movie audience, don't read a lot of novels; adults, who form the bulk of the best-seller audience, don't go to a lot of movies."[26] And both O'Toole and Bluestone cite Sartre's suggestion that for many who first experience the film, the novel is read as a commentary on the movie. If Bluestone is correct that at least in some cases, novel sales go up when an adaptation is released, and O'Toole is correct that it is probably not the film audience who are buying it, another possibility presents itself. We may be observing a confirmation that for the public the narrative is more important than the form within which it is presented. Thus the advertising for the film may lead some who won't see the film to a novel they would not otherwise consider. Bazin goes the furthest when he suggests that literature also borrows from the cinema. His reference is not to the novelization of films but to the acquisition by novelists of a new way of writing influenced by the cinema. This cinematic literature includes the hard-boiled novels of the American mystery writers, which often seem written for the screen, as well as the work of a writer like Graham Greene. Bazin argues that the cinema exists for the cinematic novelists, not as a direct source of technique, but as "a potential image." The novelists write for "a nonexistent cinema, an ideal cinema, a cinema that the novelist would produce if he were a film maker, of an imaginary art that we are still awaiting."[27]

Often the evaluation of an adaptation is complicated by the fact that what Cawelti called a mimetic (i.e., high art) novel is presented in the formulaic (i.e., generic) form of the popular

---

[26]O'Toole, <u>Film Comment</u>, November/December 1982, p. 35.

[27]Bazin, p. 62.

movie. Thus, in addition to the formal differences in the two media, the differences in audience expectation must be accounted for. These critical differences are lessened when that adaptation is based on a novel which is itself a part of a popular genre. Not only are our expectations less at odds, but the action format of popular fiction lends itself to more direct visual interpretation.

In the end we must recognize with George Bluestone that "the novel is considered less a norm than a point of departure."[28] Seeing that the film adaptation has its own integrity, its equivalence to the novel becomes one of many elements to be considered in reflecting upon it. As critics and readers familiar with both texts we will discover that our pleasure in the two texts is rooted simultaneously in their similarities and their differences.

Let us now turn our attention to the three specific adaptations which have been made of Ross Macdonald's Lew Archer novels.

4) Narrative Difference

The Moving Target and Harper

In 1965, an adaptation of Macdonald's first Lew Archer novel, The Moving Target, appeared under the title Harper. Written by William Goldman and directd by Jack Smight the film featured Paul Newman, Lauren Bacall, Pamela Tiffin, Robert Wagner, Janet Leigh, and Strother Martin.

Sixteen years separate the publication of the novel from the release of the film. The deletion of the references to World War II updates the film. In 1949, both the characters and the audience were shaped by the war years. By 1965, the war was less central to the audience's consciousness and it is not surprising that the characters' war time experiences were deleted in reworking Macdonald's original.

There are fewer narrative differences between The Moving Target and Harper than in the films made

---

[28]Bluestone, p. x.

subsequently. What changes were made are primarily simplifications which allow for fewer characters and settings in the film and which adapt the tale to the persona of the star. The most obvious change is the detective's name. Macdonald's Archer become Lew Harper, and _Harper_ takes its place with other Paul Newman vehicles such as _The Hustler_, _Hombre_, and _Hud_.

There is a significant addition at the beginning of the film. The novel opens as Acher is approaching the Sampson mansion. Harper begins several hours earlier. In a wryly comic pre-credit scene which plays against the star's handsome image, Harper awakens in his office, the TV still on from the night before. He washes his face in a basin of ice water, and brews coffee from yesterday's grounds.

That Lew Harper is living in his office prepares the viewer for a significant narrative addition--the detctive's estranged wife, Susan. The novel makes passing reference to their divorce at some time in the past.[29] In the film, Harper's refusal to accept their impending divorce becomes a recurring sub-text. When he goes to Susan battered and bleeding and tells her he will give up detecting, she allows him to stay the night. In the morning, as he leaves her to return to his case, two visual details underscore her anger and vulnerability. She stabs the yolks of the eggs she is cooking with a large fork and puts on the heavily framed glasses which, throughout the film, she has donned like a protective armor when dealing with Harper.

Given Macdonald's interests and the recurring symbolism in his novels, it is a particularly Macdonaldesque change to make the site of the ransom pick-up and Eddie Lassiter's murder an oil field and to replace the abandoned beach club where Sampson is held with an unused oil tanker. The tankers and oil field pumps belong to an industry whose violation has been a recurring image of evil in Macdonald's novels. Here the film makers have found a particualrly appropriate visual context for the novel's action.

---

[29]Macdonald, _The Moving Target_, pp. 13, 38, and 62.

The film's conclusion is shorter than the novel's. In the book, Archer enters the Sampson house with the news of Ralph Sampson's death at Albert Graves' hand and goes with Miranda to the authorities where they find that the attorney has already confessed. The film ends as Graves is unable to shoot Harper to prevent him from making his report to the Sampson women.

Change is inevitable in the process of adaptation. In Harper, the narrative changes are minimal and retain the flavor of the original novel. The additions and deletions fit the tale to the film medium, avoid the obvious time-bound elements of the original, and adapt it to the persona of its star. Lew Harper, as played by Paul Newman, is inevitably different from the Lew Archer of the novels. The detective in the film is younger, and hipper, but the changes are subtle, and Harper is an altered but recognizable Archer.

The Drowning Pool as Novel and Film

Nine years after the release of Harper, Paul Newman portrayed the detective for a second time in The Drowning Pool. Newman was co-producer and Stuart Rosenberg directed from a script by Tracy Keenan Wynn, Lorenzo Semple, Jr., and noted action writer and director Walter Hill.

There are more differences between this film and the novel on which it is based than was the case with Harper and The Moving Target. Moving the setting to the Louisiana bayou country provides a visually interesting and exotic setting and takes the detective out of his familiar, and presumably more comfortable, southern California setting. Further, the location makes it possible to cast the Devereux family (Slocums in the novel) as a part of a fading Southern aristocracy which recalls the Southern gentry of Tennessee Williams' plays.

In a move toward Hollywood convention, the film makers use romance as the source of Harper's obligation to his client. The detective and the audience discover together that the client, Mrs. James Devereux, is Harper's former lover Iris.[30]

Iris' seventeen-year-old daughter, Schuyler, has a sexual precocity and outwardly neurosis lacking in novel's fifteen-year-old Cathy. The change in her age may reflect a difference in sensibilities about what may be protrayed in a novel and on the screen. The foregrounding of the young woman's sexuality has the effect of making her relationship with the detective more aggressive and with Pat Revis less one of a child taken advantage of by an older man.

The hydrotherapy room from which the novel and film take their title is not an addition but a vividly visual setting. Here we see material from the original which lends itself to film adaptation. Their long night in the water is a unique threat, and provides an excuse to present Harper and Mavis Kibourne in a state of undress. Both Jehu's attack on Harper and the detective's subsequent escape with Mavis are visually spectacular.

As with Harper, the plot has been simplified. Several choices integrate the material into a more narrowly focused narrative. In the novel, at Revis' apartment, Kilbourne's wife Mavis seeks photographs with which she has been blackmailed. In the film she is looking for an account book listing her husband's political pay-offs. The change lessens her victimization while integrating the incident into the central issues of the plot. Similarly, by making Lieutenant Franks not only Kilbourne's informant, but the millionaire's hitman, the plot is focused and the number of characters reduced. The film offers a simpler conclusion to the tale with fewer locations than Macdonald's novel.

Given Archer's usual sexual renunciation the Macdonald fan may question making Iris and Harper former lovers. But this is typical of Hollywood's movement toward romance. The change in location makes use of a visually interesting and more exotic

---

[30]The fact that Iris is played by Newman's wife, Joanne Woodward, brings an extra-textual meaning to their relationship which would probably be known to many members of the audience.

setting than Macdonald's southern California without losing the author's characteristic use of the big oil company as a villain. The deletions and reorganizations of the plot quicken the pace and reduce the distractions, making the film a better focused retelling of the tale.

The Underground Man as Novel and Film

The Underground Man, which was published in 1971, became a made-for-TV movie in 1974 - the same year that The Drowning Pool was released in the theatres. Directed by Paul Wendkos and featuring Peter Graves as Lew Archer the film has been shown under two titles, Archer and The Underground Man, by which it is known here.

This film is far more a reflection of the California culture of its era than either of the Paul Newman vehicles. A number of changes point to the hip California of the early 1970s. While a complete catalogue of the innumerable visual objects which add to the tone of a film is of course impossible, a few should be noted. Archer himself is no longer the dark-suited detective of the novels and the Newman films. The longer haired Graves plays Archer in shorts, or slacks and a wind-breaker. The character lives in California's hip Venice artist's community. This visual data creates interesting contrasts with the seriousness of purpose which this Archer shares with the Archer of the novels.

There are a number of differences between the plots of Macdonald's novel and the Wendkos' film. While the teleplay includes the major characters, events, and motivations of the novel, some charcters are expanded, others deleted, and the number of locations reduced. Also, the order in which characters and information are presented varies from that in the novel. Finally, as with The Drowning Pool, a past romance with the mother distorts the novel's sense of obligation to the child.

Information about Jerry and Sue's pasts is simplified or drops out, as do the people from the novel who bring that information, so that both the cast and the plot are simplified. The emphasis moves from the interaction of multiple oedipal

125

secrets and searchers to focus on Stanley's dominant father search.

One major location and character are added, Cassidy's bar and its philosophical owner. Cassidy's serves as Archer's base of operations, providing male companionship and a place to receive messages. Visits to the bar bracket Archer's search for Ronny Broadhurst.

Sheriff Tremaine (played by Jack Klugman) is a minor character in the novel. Screenwriter Douglas Heyes expands this character so that Tremaine takes over much of the role of the novel's fire investigator Joe Kelsey and provides information provided by characters from the novel who are not used in the film. The sheriff and Archer have the sort of distrust combined with grudging respect which is typical of Archer's relationship with intelligent honest cops such as Ralph Knudson in The Drowning Pool and/or Sheriff Brandon Church in Macdonald's Find a Victim.

As discussed in Chapter Three, the book establishes Archer's link with Ronny Broadhurst before introducing his mother, Jean. While the possibility of a romance with Jean remains an undercurrent it is Archer's link with the boy which draws him into the case. In the film, when Ronny is brought briefly to Archer's apartment by his mother, the detective displays a stereotypical bachelor's discomfort with Ronny and shows with no sign of affection or interest in him. In the film it is wounded pride and obligation to Jean, not any tie to Ronny, which motivates Archer.

5) Conclusions

The films which have been based on the Archer novels are adaptations which reflect both Macdonald's work and the nature of film as a popular visual medium. A changing cultural context, the expectation of romance, and the particular actors who have protrayed the detective have all shaped the films. But the essential patterns, characters, and relationships of Macdonald's work remain.

What has changed in the adaptive process is the psychological and sociological subtleties of the tales. The movement toward conventional patterns of romance alters the ethical and social implications of the text. The effect of this movement, which seems common in adaptation for the screen, is to narrow and personalize the community of obligation to which the detective is responsible. This reduces the detective's ability to model a monotheistic ethic in which all people are potential sources of value and moves him from seving as a model of balanced ego integration to the narrower task of properly expressing the libido.

On the other side, it needs to be said that any adaptation involves interpretation, and there is no obligation on the part of the film makers to express this writer's interpretation of the original. The films have their own charms and meanings. The choices inherent in the adaptation of The Underground Man, for instance, advance the novel's tie with the youth culture of the time and thus make Archer's lack of interest in the boy a wry comment on the times.

BIBLIOGRAPHY

1) CRITICAL BOOKS

Allen, Dick and Chacko, David, editors. Detective
    Fiction:Crime and Compromise. New York: Harcourt
    Brace Jovanovich, 1974.

Barth, Karl. Dogmatics in Outline. New York: Harper
    & Row, 1959.

Bruccoli, Matthew S. Kenneth Millar/Ross Macdonald: A
    Checklist. Detroit: Gale Research, 1971.

Cawelti, John G. Adventure, Mystery, and Romance.
    Chicago: University of Chicago Press, 1976.

Freud, Sigmund. Beyond the Pleasure Principle. James
    Strachey, editor and translator. New York:
    W.W. Norton & Co., 1961.

_____. Civilization and Its Discontents. James
    Strachey, editor and translator. New York: W.W.
    Norton & Co., 1961.

_____. The Future of an Illusion. James Strachey,
    editor and translator. New York: W.W. Norton
    & Co., 1961.

_____. New Introductory Lectures on Psycho
    alysis. James Strachey, editor and translator. New
    York: W.W. Norton & Co., 1964.

_____. Totem and Taboo. James Strachey, editor
    and translator. New York: W.W. Norton & Co.,
    1950.

Gardiner, Dorothy, and Walker, Kathrine Sorley,
    editors. Raymond Chandler Speaking. Boston:
    Houghton Mifflin Co., 1977.

Haycraft, Howard, editor. The Art of the Mystery
    Story. New York: Simon and Schuster, 1946.

Hoedemaker, Libertus A. The Theology of H. Richard Niebuhr. New York: Pilgrim Press, 1970.

Holland, Norman. The Dynamics of Literary Response. New York: W.W. Norton & Co., 1975.

Jewett, Robert. The Captain America Complex. Santa Fe, N.M.: Bear and Co., 1984.

Jewett, Robert and Lawrence, John Shelton. The American Monomyth. New York: Doubleday, 1977.

Kaminsky, Stuart M. with Mahan, Jeffrey H. American Telvision Genres. Chicago: Nelson Hall, 1985.

Katz, Ephraim. The Film Encyclopedia. New York: Crowell, 1979.

Kitses, Jim. Horizons West. Bloomington: Indiana University Press, 1969.

Landrum, Larry M., Browne, Pat, and Browne, Ray B. editors. Dimensions of Detective Fiction. Bowling Green: Popular Press, 1976.

Laeuchli, Samuel. Religion and Art in Conflict. Philadelphia: Fortress Press, 1980.

Maddux, Rachel, Silliphant, Stirling, and Issacs, Neal D. Fiction into Film. New York: Dell, 1970.

Merton, Robert K. Social Theory and Social Structure. New York: The Free Press, 1968.

Most, Glenn W. and Stowe, William, W. editors. The Poetics of Murder. New York: Harcourt Brace Jovanovich, 1983.

Nelson, John Wiley. Your God is Alive and Well and Appearing in Popular Culture. Philadelphia: Westminster Press, 1976.

Nevins, Francis M. Jr., editor. The Mystery Writer's Art. Bowling Green: Popular Press, 1970.

Niebuhr, H. Richard. Christ and Culture. New York: Harper Colophon, 1975.

_____. The Meaning of Revelation. New York: Macmillian Pub. Co., Inc., 1941.

_____. *Radical Monotheism and Western Culture*. New York: Harper Torchbooks, 1975.

_____. *The Responsible Self*. New York: Harper and Row, 1963.

Niebuhr, Reinhold. *Moral Man and Immoral Society*. New York: Charles Scribner's Sons, 1960.

Nye, Russell B. *The Unembarrassed Muse*. New York: Dial Press, 1970.

Ottati, Douglas F. *Meaning and Method in H. Richard Niebuhr's Theology*. Washington, D.C.: University Press of America, 1982.

Scott, Nathan. *The Broken Center: Studies in the Theological Horizon of Modern Literature*. New Haven: Yale University Press, 1966.

_____. *Craters of the Spirit: Studies in the Modern Novel*. Washington: Corpus Books, 1968.

_____. *Modern Literature and the Religious Frontier*. New York: Harper and Row, 1968.

Speir, Jerry. *Ross Macdonald*. New York: Fredrick Ungar, 1978.

Wolfe, Peter, *Dreamers Who Live Their Dreams*. Bowling Green: Popular Press, 1976.

2 - FICTION

Chandler, Raymond. *The High Window*. New York: Vintage Books, 1976.

_____. *The Midnight Raymond Chandler*. Boston: Houghton Mifflin Co., 1971.

Hammett, Dashiell. *The Maltese Falcon*. New York: Vintage Books, 1972.

_____. *Red Harvest*. New York: Alfred A. Knopf, 1929.

_____. *The Thin Man*. New York: Alfred A. Knopf, 1934.

Kaminsky, Stuart M. _Bullet for a Star_. New York: Saint Martin's Press, 1977.

Kotzwinkle, William, _ET: The Extraterrestial_. New York: Putnam, 1985.

Macdonald, John, [Kenneth Millar]. _The Moving Target_. New York: Alfred A. Knopf, 1949.

Macdonald, John Ross, [Kenneth Millar]. _The Drowning Pool_. New York: Alfred A. Knopf, 1950.

_____. _Find a Victim_. New York: Alfred A. Knopf, 1950.

_____. _The Ivory Grin_. New York: Alfred A. Knopf, 1954.

_____. _Meet Me at the Morgue_. New York: Alfred A. Knopf, 1953.

_____. _The Way Some People Die_. New York: Alfred A. Knopf, 1951.

_____. _The Way Some People Die_. New York: Pocket Books, 1952.

Macdonald Ross, [Kenneth Millar]. _The Barbarous Coast_. New York: Knopf, 1956.

_____. _Black Money_. New York: Alfred A. Knopf, 1966.

_____. _The Blue Hammer_. New York: Alfred A. Knopf, 1976.

_____. _The Chill_. New York: Alfred A. Knopf, 1964.

_____. _The Doomsters_. New York: Alfred A. Knopf, 1958.

_____. _The Drowning Pool_. New York: Alfred A. Knopf, 1970.

_____. _The Far Side of the Dollar_. New York: Knopf, 1965.

_____. _The Ferguson Affair_. New York: Alfred A. Knopf, 1960.

_____. The Galton Case. New York: Alfred A. Knopf, 1959.

_____. The Goodbye Look. New York: Alfred A. Knopf, 1969.

_____. The Instant Enemy. New York: Alfred A. Knopf, 1968.

_____. The Moving Target. New York: Alfred A. Knopf, 1979.

_____. Sleeping Beauty. New York: Alfred A. Knopf, 1973.

_____. The Underground Man. New York: Alfred A. Knopf, 1971.

_____. The Underground Man. New York: Bantam, 1972.

_____. The Wycherly Woman. New York: Alfred A. Knopf, 1961.

_____. The Zebra-Striped Hearse. New York: Alfred A. Knopf, 1962.

Kenneth Millar. Blue City. New York: Alfred A. Knopf, 1947.

_____. The Dark Tunnel. New York: Alfred A. Knopf, 1944.

_____. The Three Roads. New York: Alfred A. Knopf, 1948.

_____. Trouble Follows Me. New York: Alfred A. Knopf, 1946.

McClure, James. Blood of an Englishman. New York: Pantheon, 1972.

_____. Caterpiller Cop. New York: Panteon, 1980.

_____. Steam Pig. New York: Pantheon, 1980.

Paretsky, Sara. Deadlock. New York: Ballantine Books, 1984.

_____. _Indemnity Only_. New York: Ballantine Books, 1982.

Sjowall, Maj and Wahloo, Per. _The Abominable Man_. Thomas Teal, translator. New York: Vintage Books, 1980.

_____. _Cop Killer_. Thomas Teal, translator. New York: Vintage Books, 1978.

_____. _Roseanna_. Lois Roth, translator. New York: Bantam, 1967.

Soloman, Brad. _Open Shadow_. New York: Avon, 1978.

3) ARTICLES AND PERIODICALS

Berkman, Ed. "Superheroes, Antiheroes, and the Heroism Void in Children's Television," _The Christian Century_, XCVI (July 4-11, 1979), 704ff.

Chandler, Raymond. "The Simple Art of Murder," in _The Simple Art of Murder_ New York: Ballantine Books, 1972. 1-21.

Clemons, Walter. "Ross Macdonald at His Best," _New York Times_ (Feb. 9, 1971), Book Section, 33.

Combs, William W. "The Detective as Both Tortoise and Achilles," _Clues_, II (Spring/Summer 1981), 98-105.

Cook, Bruce. "The Prince in the Poorhouse," _The Catholic World_ (October 1971), 27ff.

Durham, Philip. "The Black Mask School," _The Mystery Writer's Art_ Francis M. Nevins, Jr., editor. Bowling Green: Popular Press, 1970. 197-225.

Fishman, Charles. "Another Peacock Cry: Heraldic Birds in Five Lew Archer Novels," _Clues_, II (Spring/Summer 1981), 106-115.

Forshey, Gerald E. "The Apocalyptic Mood in Contemporary Film," _explor_, IV (Spring 1978), 28-37.

_____. "Studies in Religion and Popular Culture," _explor_, VII (Fall 1984), 17-27.

Freud, Sigmund. "Creative Writers and Day-dreaming," The Standard Edition of the Complete Psychoanalytic Works, IX, Toronto: Hogarth Press, 1960, 140-154.

Grogg, Sam Jr. "Ross Macdonald: At the Edge," Journal of Popular Culture, II (Summer 1973), 215ff.

Gella, George. "Murder and the Mean Streets:The Hard-boiled Detective Story," Detective Fiction: Crime and Compromise, D. Allen and D. Chacko, editors. New York: Harcourt Brace Jovanovich, 1974, 387-398.

Hagemann, E. R., editor. "Focus on Pulp Detective Fiction," Clues, II (Fall/Winter 1981), 38-153.

Lawrence, John Shelton, "A Critical Analysis of Roger B. Rollins' 'Against Evaluation'," Journal of Popular Culture, XII (Summer 1978), 110ff.

Lingeman, Richard, "The Underground Bye-Bye," New York Times (June 6, 1971), Sec. 7, 61.

Mahan, Jeffrey H. "The Hard-boiled Detective in the Fallen World," Clues, I (Fall/Winter 1980), 90-98.

_____. "Once Upon a Time in the West," explor, VII (Fall 1984), 81-93.

Osborne, David. "John Sayles - Hoboken to Hollywood and Back," American Film (October 1982), 31ff.

O'Toole, Lawrence. "Now Read the Movie," Film Comment (November/December 1982), 34ff.

Pry, Elmer. "Lew Archer's Moral Universe," Dimesnions of Detective Fiction, L. Landrum, P. Browne, and R. Browne, editors. Bowling Green: Popular Press, 1976, 174-181.

Schickel, Richard. "The Underground Man," Commentary (September 1971), 96ff.

Welty, Eudora. "The Stuff Nightmares Are Made Of," New York Times (February 4, 1971), Book Section, 7.

4) UNPUBLISHED MATERIAL

Abrahams, Etta Claire. "Vision and Values in the Action Detective Novel: A Study of Raymond Chandler, Kenneth Millar (Ross Macdonald) and John D. MacDonald," Unpublished Ph.D. dissertation, Michigan State University, 1973.

Crider, Allen Billy, "The Private Eye hero: A Study of Dashiell Hammett, Raymond Chandler, and Ross Macdonald," Unpublished Ph.D. dissertation, University of Texas at Austin, 1972.

INDEX

Fleming, I., 26

Forshey, G., xiv, xv

Francis, D., 3

Freud, S., xx, 17f, 91, 93
  Civilization and its Discontents, 19, 20, 50
  "Creative Writers and Day-dreaming," 23, 24, 30
  Future of an Illusion, 17, 19
  New Intro Lectures..., 33, 34
  Totem and Taboo, 21, 35

Goldman, W., 121

Graves, P., 125

Greene, G., 119, 120

Grella, G., xxii, 11, 15

Gustafson, J., 53

Hammett, D., xi, 2, 3, 14, 26, 28, 64
  Maltese Falcon, 3, 5, 8, 13, 14, 55, 59, 64
  Red Harvest, 96

Harper (film), 60, 76, 110, 121f

Haycraft, H., xxii

Hemingway, E., 116

Hill, W., 123

Hoedemaker, L. A., 53, 55, 59, 60

Holland, N., x, xi, 25, 32, 95, 96

Issacs, N.D., 116

Jewett, R., xiii, xv

Jewett, R., & J. S. Lawrence, xv, 45

Journal of Popular Culture, xii

Jung, C.G., 21

Kaminsky, S. M., 5

Kaminsky, S. & J. H. Mahan, 32

Kinski, N., 106

Klugman, J. 126

Laeuchli, S., xiii

LeCarre, J., 26

Leigh, J., 121

MacDonald, J.D., 26

Macdonald, R.,
  Barbarous Coast, v, 5
  Drowning Pool, 5, 66, 121f
  Moving Target, 6, 18, 20, 27-30, 37, 38, 40-48,
  93, 121f
  Sleeping Beauty, 66
  Underground Man, 43, 53, 57, 61, 62, 64, 67,
  70,   71, 73, 76, 77, 81-87, 89, 98, 108-110,
  125f
  Way Some People Die, 6, 48

Maddux, R., 116

Mahan, J. H., xvi, 48

Martin, S., 121

Merton, R. K., xx

Miller, G., 111

Millar, K., xxii

Montgomery, R., 109

Most, G. W. & W. W. Stowe, xxii

Nelson, J. W., xv

Neuman, P., 106, 122, 123

Proust, M., 118

Niebuhr, H. R., xx, 53f, 91, 102
  Christ and Culture, 68, 87, 89, 93
  Meaning of Revelation, 62